The Church and the Older Person

The Church
and the Older Person

by

Robert M. Gray   and   David O. Moberg
University of Utah, Salt Lake City   *Bethel College, St. Paul, Minnesota*

with a Foreword by
ERNEST W. BURGESS
Professor Emeritus of Sociology, University of Chicago

William B. Eerdmans Publishing Company
Grand Rapids, Michigan

First printing, February 1962
Second printing, November 1963
Third printing, June 1968

PHOTOLITHOPRINTED BY GRAND RAPIDS BOOK MANUFACTURERS, INC.
GRAND RAPIDS, MICHIGAN, UNITED STATES OF AMERICA
1968

FOREWORD

THIS BOOK on the place and function of religion in the lives of older persons is the first to be solidly based on the findings of social science research. Dr. Gray and Dr. Moberg present the known facts about aging and the religious behavior and experiences of older persons. They also include their own original contributions which measurably advance our knowledge of the meaning of religion in the lives of the aging.

Certain findings of the authors furnish guideposts to ministers and to all others interested in the welfare of older persons. Church membership in and of itself seems not to be related to good personal adjustments, but religious beliefs and activities probably are. Interviews reveal concretely how religion and the church function in satisfying the basic needs of older persons and in enabling them to face and meet the problems of old age such as fear of death, loneliness, the loss of the spouse and other crises.

These interviews also disclosed the conflict in roles between the older and the younger church members and the feeling of the former that they are being rejected. The older members are also dissatisfied with their inability to contribute to the church, to dress appropriately, to meet the cost of transportation to services and with the changes in the church from the good old ways of the past.

The recommendations made by the authors will be of value to ministers, other religious workers and older people. Suggestions are made of ways in which the church can fulfill its obligations to its older members; but also, and of equal if not greater importance, are specifications indicating how older people can be of help to the church.

One puzzling question is not conclusively answered by this volume. It is the explanation of the greater religiosity of older people than of middle-aged and younger people in this country. The experiences associated with aging as described in this book may be sufficient reason. But this consideration does not rule out cultural survivals in the present generation of older persons of the religious beliefs and convictions of their child-hood and youth.

A valuable appendix contains suggestions for further re-search. They cover a wide range — church members compared with non-members, evaluation of existing types of church pro-grams, differences between church members by social class, impact of urbanization upon the church and its older mem-bers, religious conflict and personal adjustment in old age, per-sonal satisfactions derived from religion and the church, self-selection of religious faith and activity, non-Christian religions and personal adjustment in old age, religious and personal adjustment in the stages of the cycle of adjustment, adaptability in old age, the pervasiveness of religion in old age, the "faith of our fathers" and personal adjustment, church leadership and personal adjustment, church participation compared with other social participation, the status of older persons in the church, the church and the needs of older people, religious conversions of older people, fluctuations in their personal adjustment, re-ligious beliefs of older people, and international comparisons. These suggestions may well stimulate research which will throw new light upon the many ways in which religion makes its distinctive contribution to the welfare and happiness of older persons.

ERNEST W. BURGESS
Professor Emeritus of Sociology
University of Chicago

PREFACE

MUCH SYSTEMATIC RESEARCH AND STUDY and many practical programs relating to the church and older people have been introduced in the past decade. This book is a survey of present knowledge about the church and older people in contemporary American society, chiefly from the viewpoint of modern social science. The general objective of the present work has been to contribute to systematization in this area by the coordination and integration of current pertinent research efforts of several disciplines concerning this problem.

Perhaps this book can most accurately be thought of as a work in applied social science. Not only is empirical knowledge as related to accumulated theory presented, but suggestions which flow out of that knowledge are given to churches and to older people. An attempt has been made to present all the material in a way that will interest them as well as social scientists. Suggestions for further research proposed by this study have therefore been placed in the appendix. Technical details have been simplified or referred to in footnotes through which the interested scholar may find them.

As social scientists, the authors believe that they are not circumventing their professional role by stepping into the position of suggesting and recommending certain types of activity. Rather they are helping to implement the cooperation between science and the practicing professions which is increasingly recognized as essential to the welfare of society and which Donald Young, President of the American Sociological Society in 1955, declared in his presidential address to be so important.

It is obvious from the footnotes in the text that certain chapters are more the work of one author than the other. This book is nevertheless an outgrowth of cooperative planning and true collaboration in which each has revised and re-written the work of the other. In other words, both are equally responsible for all parts of the book.

A large number of people have contributed to the development of the book in various ways. It is not possible to mention here all those who aided, in one way or another, in its preparation. Special gratitude is due to the readers of preliminary manuscripts of this work, who gave many valuable suggestions for its improvement. They are the Reverend Warren Magnuson, Pastor of the Central Baptist Church in St. Paul, Minnesota; the Reverend Joseph E. Tanquist, retired missionary to Assam, India; the Reverend Lynn S. Lyon, Pastor of Salt Lake City's Central Christian Church and past President of the Salt Lake Ministerial Association; Dr. Lloyd Wilcox, Chairman, Department of Social Science, Westminster College, Salt Lake City, Utah; Dr. Rex. A. Skidmore, Dean, Graduate School of Social Work, Dr. Henry Frost, Chairman, Department of Sociology, and Dr. Anthon Cannon, Professor of Sociology, all of the University of Utah.

We are also grateful to many other friends and colleagues who have directly or indirectly contributed to this work. Among those to whom special recognition is due are Dr. Clifford E. Larson, Dean of Bethel College; Dr. F. Stuart Chapin, Professor Emeritus of the University of Minnesota; Dr. Ernest W. Burgess, Professor Emeritus of the University of Chicago; John K. Edmunds, President of the Chicago Stake, Church of Jesus Christ of Latter-day Saints; the Reverend Adolph Bohn of the Edgewater Beach Presbyterian Church, Chicago, Illinois; the Reverend Virgil Lowder, formerly of the Church Federation of Greater Chicago, and Dr. Lauris B. Whitman and Dr. Benson Y. Landis of the Bureau of Research and Survey, National Council of Churches, New York City.

Finally, our sincere appreciation is extended to our wives, Helen Hale and Helen H., for their generous sympathy and understanding during the course of the study. Without their comfort and hard work this book would not have been possible.

—R. M. G. and D. O. M.

CONTENTS

CHAPTER 1

INTRODUCTION

"THE PROBLEM OF OLD AGE" has become a common expression. In the contemporary church, just as in social and recreational organizations, academic institutions, and business and industrial establishments, attention is often turned to questions of the social, economic, spiritual and mental well-being of older people.

The social problems connected with old age tend to undermine the dignity and the sense of personal worth of the older person. Americans are increasingly aware of the fact that the problems of old age have economic, social and psychological consequences for everyone in our nation, whether aging or old. The growing sensitivity to the fact that the widespread practice of relegating the aged to a place of disrespect and contempt is inconsistent with democratic ideals has helped to focus attention on the problem of old age.

The number of people affected by the problems of old age and retirement in America is far greater than the number directly affected by the traditional types of crime and juvenile delinquency that have been the subject matter of many college and university courses. In the United States there are about six times as many persons past their sixty-fifth birthdays as there are either divorcees or college students. The aged also far outnumber many ethnic and racial minority groups that have received considerable attention from scholars. Yet it is only recently that social scientists have turned their attention to the systematic study of old age.

Both the increasing number of old people in our population and the increasing emphasis upon the place of religion in the lives of individuals and in the affairs of society make an examination of the relationship between the older person and the church especially pertinent and appropriate today. Churches, in cooperation with other agencies and institutions, are trying to meet many of the needs presented by the problems of the aged. There is a need to survey the effectiveness of their programs and to suggest additional ways in which they can improve their work.

It is more than a decade since Otto Pollak wrote that the impact of the various aspects of religious life upon the adjustment problems of old age had almost completely escaped the attention of social scientists. "This neglect," he said, "is surprising because phenomena associated with old age always have aroused the anxiety of man and thus created a special need for comfort and reassurance, which throughout the ages have come from the sources of religion."[1] The questions asked by Pollak and the Social Science Research Council's committee on social adjustment in old age have stimulated much research; today at least tentative answers may be given to many of the questions they raised.

WHO IS AN OLDER PERSON?

To say that an older person is one who has reached old age seems like a simple, uncontroversial, commonplace statement. The term "old age," however, is often used very loosely. One must know the context in which it appears in order to interpret its use correctly.

There are at least three reasons for the lack of a clear-cut definition of what constitutes old age. One is the relativity of old age. Professional baseball players, boxers, and football stars are "old" by the age of thirty or thirty-five years; but President Eisenhower at the age of sixty-five in 1956 was not considered too old for election to a second term as President of the United States. Sir Winston Churchill did not retire as Prime Minister in England until he had passed his eightieth birthday, yet many an American clergyman has been prematurely "laid on the shelf" at the age of fifty or fifty-five. The profession or occupation of an individual often dictates the age at which he becomes "old"; this age varies tremendously from one occupation to another.

---

1. Otto Pollak, *Social Adjustment in Old Age*, Social Science Research Council, Bulletin 59, 1948, p. 161. See also C. Fleming, "Needed — A Social Philosophy for the Problems of Aging," *Geriatrics*, 10:549-551, Nov., 1955.

Difficulties of defining "old age" also result from the relative positions from which judgments are made. The grade school child is likely to consider high school students to be old and mature. The college student often regards married persons who have children as old. Even upon arrival at the "ripe old age" of seventy or more, others of the same age appear young to the person making the comparison.

A third source of differences in the definition of old age is the tremendous variation in individual characteristics. The superintendent of a home for retired and disabled veterans once told one of the authors of a thirty year old man whose outward appearance made him seem as old as certain of the oldest residents in his institution, some of whom were over one hundred years of age. Many people at the age of sixty-five or seventy can pass among strangers as being twenty years younger, while others in their fifties or sixties are thought to be aged eighty-five or ninety. The process of aging does not affect all alike. One person is "old" at fifty, while another is still "young" at seventy-five. Many a rural church has gray-haired members in its young peoples society!

For most purposes, precise definition of "old age" is unimportant. At times, however, it becomes necessary to assign older persons to or take them away from certain positions. Retirement policies even for church-related jobs are often based in part upon definitions of old age. Scientists also need precise definitions as they conduct their research. There are four major types of potentially usable definitions: the physiological, psychological, sociological and chronological.

Physiologically a person is old when the signs of wearing out of the body appear. There is much disagreement among biological and medical authorities as to the time at which this senescence[2] normally begins. There is no one age when all physical functions of a given individual begin to show a decline. Deterioration of the various parts of the body proceeds at different rates of change and generally is so slow that it cannot be measured accurately at weekly, monthly or even annual intervals. Not all indications of age appear with equal severity in a given individual. Except for certain limited purposes it

2. *Senescence* refers to normal old age in which the physical condition of gradual deterioration of the body is apparent; in contrast, *senility* is used increasingly to refer primarily to the abnormal mental conditions that occur in old age.

is therefore not yet practicable to use physiological criteria as a basis for determining whether or not an individual is "old."[3]

Psychological definitions of old age are based on changing mental abilities, such as memory and intelligence, changing attitudes and changing emotional reactions. Here again there is no one age when all individuals begin to show the signs of aging. The rate of change is very slow and difficult to measure, and there are internal differences for a given individual in the appearance of the various signs of aging as well as in the rate at which they proceed. It is not feasible at present to use psychological criteria as a practical basis for determining who is old because the problems of measurement have not yet been surmounted.[4]

From a *sociological* viewpoint, a person is old when he has relinquished the social relationships, roles, and statuses which are typical of middle-aged adulthood and accepted those which are more typical of persons in the later years of life. In "primitive" societies it is relatively easy to classify persons in this way, for in them definite active roles, such as preparation of food and clothing, midwifery, ceremonial leadership, and the like, have been assigned to older people. In modern urbanized America, however, there is no definite place established for the aged, and as a result we cannot define old age precisely on the basis of sociological criteria.[5]

3. For discussions of physiological definitions of old age see Ruth S. Cavan, Ernest W. Burgess, Robert J. Havighurst, and Herbert Goldhamer, *Personal Adjustment in Old Age,* Science Research Associates, 1949, pp. 2-4; Anton J. Carlson and Edward J. Stieglitz, "Physiological Changes in Aging," *Annals of the American Academy of Political and Social Science,* 279:18-31, Jan., 1952; I. M. Murray, "Assessment of Physiologic Age by Combination of Several Criteria — Vision, Hearing, Blood Pressure, and Muscle Force," *Journal of Gerontology,* 6:120-126, Apr., 1951; and Arthur T. Todd, *Medical Aspects of Growing Old,* John Wright and Sons, Ltd., 1946, pp. 8, *passim.*

4. Psychological definitions of old age are discussed in L. Pearl Gardner, "Attitudes and Activities of the Middle-Aged and Aged," *Geriatrics,* 4:33-50, Jan.-Feb., 1949; Oscar J. Kaplan, "Psychological Aspects of Aging," *Annals of the American Academy of Political and Social Science,* 279:32-42, Jan., 1952, and Lawrence F. Greenleigh, *Changing Psychological Concepts of Aging,* Washington, D. C., National Institute of Health, U. S. Dept. of Health, Education, and Welfare, 1953.

5. See Ruth S. Cavan *et al., op. cit.,* pp. 6-8; Leo W. Simmons, *The Role of the Aged in Primitive Society,* Yale University Press, 1945; Edward Nelson Palmer, "Toward a Sociological Definition of Old Age: A Research Note," *American Journal of Sociology,* 59:28-29, July, 1953; and Esther H. Penchef, "The Concept of Social Age," *Sociology and Social Research,* 34:177-183, Jan.-Feb., 1950.

Because of the difficulties of using these definitions, *chronological* age is the standard used by most who speak or write about it.   Although age in years has varying significance for different individuals, many positions people fill in society are determined in part by their chronological age.   A person's physiological, psychological, and sociological old age are related to his chronological age.

In this book the term *older person* refers to one who is chronologically "up in years."   It applies primarily to senescent individuals who are experiencing "normal" old age; only incidental reference will be made to those who are physically, mentally and socially incompetent and infirm.

There are limitations in such word usage.   Many chronologically old persons are "young" in body, mind and social relationships.   Old age in any one sphere of life is not necessarily accompanied by old age in the others.   Not everyone who is above the age of sixty or sixty-five has economic, social, or personal problems, and not everyone who is old constitutes a problem for the church and the rest of society.

THE CHURCH AND THE OLDER PERSON

The local church and its membership and program is the chief subject of this book's discussion of the church.   Although this book deals primarily with older people and the Christian religion, much of the content applies directly to Judaism and other religions in America as well.   This is particularly true of the recommendations summarized in Chapters 8 and 9.

The specific activities a church can undertake for older people are related to its theological and philosophical orientation, the age-structure of the community it serves, the activities of the rest of society on behalf of the aged, the value-judgments of its members, and numerous other factors.

The historical traditions of some churches prevent them from putting certain methods of serving older people into practice. In some cases, doctrinal interpretations may prevent the application of recommended activities.   For example, if Holy Communion is looked upon as a sacrament that imparts a measure of special grace to those who partake of it, the serving of Communion to the ill and to shut-ins is likely to be considered an essential part of the ministry of its clergy.   If, on the other hand, the Lord's Supper is believed to be an ordinance of the church with only symbolic significance, the administration of Communion to an older person alone in his home or in the hospital and not in the literal presence of fellowshiping believers may be considered unnecessary or even improper.

The church that is located in a community where *all* the social, recreational, economic and similar needs of older people are already being met effectively through special clubs, recreational centers, counseling facilities, and other agencies may not need to do much more for older people than to continue its traditional program of worship and Christian teaching. Such communities, needless to say, are very rare if not nonexistent!

Biased opinions of members of the church (such as some of those we shall examine in a later chapter) may limit the scope of its activities for the aged. Wise leadership over an extended period of time can do much to modify these biases in a direction consistent with the basic values of the religious faith the church represents. In planning programs to meet the challenge of older people, these biases must not be ignored, since they may prove to be the downfall of an otherwise excellent plan.

Coordination and integration of the efforts of churchmen and representatives of various scientific disciplines interested in the problems and the relationships of the church and the older person hold great promise for better theoretical understanding and improved programs of action. Among the subjects about which increased knowledge is needed are the problems of specific types or categories of older people, their religious beliefs and practices, actual and potential contributions of the church to the aged, and contributions of older people to the church. Additional information about the effects of each of these upon older people is especially needed.

Tentative answers for numerous questions which may be asked about the relationships between the church and the older person are found in this book. A listing of some of these questions follows.

What are the problems of older people in America about which the church ought to be concerned? How does the church sometimes create or contribute to the problems of the aged? Why do many oldsters feel that they are being pushed aside in the church in favor of younger members? Are they really being pushed aside? Do any older church members stay away from church services because they are unable to make

financial contributions or because they think they cannot
dress well enough to attend?

Are the religious beliefs and activities of older people different from those of youths and young adults? Do people have
increased need for religious faith and practices in old age?
Do old people think they have lost prestige and authority
(status and power) in the church? Has their position actually
been lowered?

Do "religious" people have better personal adjustment in
old age than the non-religious? How do one's religious beliefs and activities affect him in old age? How are church
membership, religious activities, and lay leadership in the
church related to well-being in the closing years of life? Is
the person who is closely integrated into the church in a more
favorable position in old age than the one who is only on the
fringes of the church fellowship or not in the church at all?
How do church experiences affect the anxiety caused by the
thought of approaching death?

In what ways does the church make a contribution to older
persons? How does it satisfy the basic needs of the aged? What
does the church do to relieve the elderly person's feelings
of loneliness and being unwanted? How does it offer support
to its members in times of difficulty and crisis? How can
church activities furnish an outlet for one's need to participate
in a social environment in which he feels welcome? What
does it mean to the oldster that church leaders and members
continue to be interested in and to visit him even after his
relatives, other friends and associates may have discontinued
doing so? How can the church do more to assist its members
who are making the transition from middle age to later maturity? What else can it do for older people?

What can older people do for the church? How do the
services they offer the church hinder or help their own personal
adjustment? How do they assess their experiences in the
church?

What limitations upon present knowledge of the church
and the older person can serve as guideposts for further experimentation, study and research by church workers and social scientists? (Because this is a specialized subject, the organized presentation of it is in Appendix II.)

*   *   *

The next chapter is a discussion of some of the problems
commonly experienced by older persons in America. This is

followed by a summary of numerous studies of older people which include reference to their religious beliefs and activities. Chapters 4 through 7 present the findings of two research projects which were oriented specifically around the problems of old age in relation to religion and the church.   The two concluding chapters summarize practical suggestions for the church and the older person.   The first appendix consists of the basic policy statements and recommendations of the Section on Religion of the 1961 White House Conference on Aging.   The second appendix consists of suggestions for further study for the use of those who would like to know some of the limitations of present knowledge and unexplored topics worthy of experimentation and research.

CHAPTER 2

PROBLEMS OF OLDER PEOPLE

A REVOLUTION IN POPULATION CHARACTERISTICS closely followed
the industrial revolution in western Europe and the United
States. One of the outstanding results of this demographic
revolution has been a shift in the age composition of the population. During the century following 1850 the proportion of
persons aged 50 to 59 years in the U. S. more than doubled,
those from 60 to 69 nearly trebled, and the proportion of people
aged 70 years and over increased by more than three times.[1]

During the half century from 1900 to 1950 the population
of the United States doubled, but the number of persons past
age 65 quadrupled. In 1900 only one in every twenty-five persons in our total population was aged 65 years or over; in 1950
the ratio was one in twelve and steadily decreasing.[2] In the
single decade 1940 to 1950 the population above the age of
65 increased by thirty-seven per cent while the number at ages
under 65 increased by only thirteen per cent.[3] By 1975 our
population aged 65 and over will, according to Bureau of the
Census estimates, be about seventy per cent higher than it
was in 1950. At that time a total of 21,872,000 persons, 9.3

1. Clark Tibbitts and Henry D. Sheldon, "Introduction: A Philosophy
of Aging," *Annals of the American Academy of Political and Social Science,*
279:1-10, Jan., 1952.

2. Committee on Aging and Geriatrics, Federal Security Agency, *Fact
Book on Aging,* U. S. Government Printing Office, 1952, p. 4.

3. "Our Aged and What They Do," *Statistical Bulletin,* Metropolitan
Life Insurance Co., Vol. 32, No. 7, p. 5, July, 1951. From 1950 to 1960
the population aged 65 and over increased by 34.7 per cent to a total of
16,559,580, of whom 55 per cent were women. (Special Staff on Aging,
Dept. of Health, Education, and Welfare, *New Population Facts on Older
Americans,* 1960, U. S. Government Printing Office, 1961, pp. 2-4.)

per cent of our anticipated total population, will be in this older age category, compared with 12,271,000 in 1950.[4]

It was in part a realization of these population trends that made churchmen, social scientists, and others hold many conferences on the needs of the aged. Special courses on geriatrics and gerontology have been introduced to the curricula of colleges and universities, research has been done on the subject, books have been written, a host of articles have appeared in both popular and scholarly journals, and new popular magazines for older people as well as scholarly journals in the fields of geriatrics and gerontology have been issued. It is universally recognized by those who have devoted careful attention to the subject that older people have numerous problems even in the United States, the most prosperous large nation on earth.

Some of the problems faced by the aged are an almost inevitable result of the physiological and psychological changes that result from the aging process. Others are largely a result of man's dealings with his fellowmen; these can be alleviated most readily by wise and considerate programs of the church, the government, and other social institutions and organizations.

The older person in the United States typically faces problems that are more numerous, more serious and more strange to him than any he has faced since his adolescence and early adulthood. The stereotyped picture of grandmother sitting at ease in her rocking chair all day with no worries or cares whatever is not characteristic of the majority of American grandmothers. For most people, old age is a period of development and adjustment "rather than a period of nirvana — of blissful and unstriving ease leading to a quiet and peaceful passing out of this life."[5]

The picture of the aged man drawn in *As You Like It* by William Shakespeare was no doubt a conception typical of the pictures of the aged citizen in the minds of many of his countrymen:

> *All the world's a stage,*
> *And all the men and women merely players;*
> *They have their exits and their entrances,*

4. Bureau of the Census, "Illustrative Projections of the Population of the United States, by Age and Sex, 1960 to 1980," *Current Population Reports*, Series P-25, No. 187, Nov. 10, 1958, pp. 16-17. (The percentage is based on Series II; it could be over 10 per cent if Series IV proves the better projection.)

5. Robert J. Havighurst, "Old Age — An American Problem," *Journal of Gerontology*, 4:300, Oct., 1949.

And one man in his time plays many parts,
His acts being seven ages. . . .
                              The sixth age shifts
Into the lean and slippered pantaloon,
With spectacles on nose, and pouch on side;
His youthful hose well saved, a world too wide
For his shrunk shanks; and his big manly voice,
Turning again towards childish treble, pipes
And whistles in his sound. Last scene of all
That ends this strange eventful history,
Is second childishness, and mere oblivion:
Sans teeth, sans eyes, sans taste, sans everything.

Perhaps in Shakespeare's day, just as today, the stereotyped picture of the old man did not fit the majority of older people; yet there are some elements of truth in the physical and mental characteristics implied in his statement. The physical and mental changes which often accompany old age, whether first apparent at the age of forty or at the age of eighty, take place within a cultural setting which determines their significance and which, in our country, decrees almost inevitably that there shall be economic and social problems as well. We shall, therefore, examine briefly some of the typical physical, economic, psychological, social and spiritual problems faced by older persons here and in other nations with cultures similar to ours. All of these problems have distinct implications, implicitly or explicitly, for the church and its work.

PHYSICAL PROBLEMS[6]

Both the belief that old age is necessarily a period of deterioration and that there are certain diseases which are the special province of old age alone are false. It is true, however, that the effects of many diseases upon older people differ radically from the effects of the same diseases upon the young.

Although almost everyone who lives to the age of sixty has acquired some more or less permanent disability or disease,

6. The factual details in this section, except where otherwise noted, are based upon the report of The President's Commission on the Health Needs of the Nation, *Building America's Health,* U. S. Government Printing Office, 1953, Vol. II, "America's Health Status, Needs and Resources," pp. 89ff., and Vol. III, "America's Health Status, Needs and Resources — A Statistical Appendix," pp. 125ff. Cf. the Hearings Before the Subcommittee on Problems of the Aged and Aging of the Committee on Labor and Public Welfare, U. S. Senate, 86th Congress, Second Session, *Health Needs of the Aged and Aging,* U.S. Government Printing Office, 1960.

only about ten to fifteen per cent of the elderly are actually in-
capacitated at any one time. About one man in every seven
aged sixty and over is hospitalized in the course of a year. The
National Health Survey found that persons aged sixty-five and
over were confined to bed by illness and accidents an average
of 16.3 days and restricted in their activities for 47.3 days during the year ended June 30, 1958. A clinical survey in Balti-
more revealed that only one in every twenty-two persons aged
sixty-five and over was free of chronic disease; in six cases out
of seven the disease interfered with or limited daily activities
or required care. Over half of the older people examined had
arthritis, and nearly three-fifths had some form of heart disease.
The illnesses of the aged are more frequent than those of
younger adults, and they also tend to be of longer duration.[7]

Many elderly people are faced with the problem of adjustment to their own or their spouse's disability, and frequently
they are invalids for prolonged periods of time before death
relieves them of their suffering. As Havighurst has indicated,
half of all who live to be over the age of fifty die of heart disease or its complications; this comes on slowly and first makes
one an invalid in a substantial proportion of cases. Fully one-
half of those who reach the age of seventy can expect several
years of invalidism before death.[8]

A large proportion of deaths in the U. S. today occur among
persons over the age of sixty-five. In 1900 about one-fourth
of all deaths occurred among the four per cent of the population in the older years, while in 1950 over half of all deaths
were among the eight per cent of the population in the same
age group.[9] The advances of the medical sciences have made
it possible for thousands to avoid being stricken by or to survive
the results of diseases that would otherwise have taken their
lives at an earlier age.

In the U. S. in 1950, as a reflection chiefly of the high death
rates of the aged together with the tendency of men to marry
younger mates and to die at an earlier age than women, over

7. "Hospitalization of Men at Ages 60 and Over," *Statistical Bulletin,*
Vol. 36, No. 5, pp. 1-3, May, 1955, and "Health Problems in Later Life,"
Statistical Bulletin, Vol. 40, No. 3, pp. 6-8, Mar., 1959.
8. Robert J. Havighurst, *op. cit.,* pp. 298-304.
9. In 1957, 938,294 or 57.05 per cent of all deaths in continental U. S.
occurred to persons aged 65 and over. ("Mortality from Selected Causes...,
1957," *Vital Statistics — Special Reports, National Summaries,* Vol. 50, No.
5, Apr. 24, 1959.)

half (55.3 per cent) of all women aged sixty-five years and over were widowed, while just over one-third (36.0 per cent) were married, and the remainder were divorced or single. Approximately one-fourth (23.6 per cent) of the men in the same age category were widowed, while two-thirds (66.2 per cent) were married, and one-tenth (10.2 per cent) were single or divorced.

With increasing age there is a general reduction in strength, endurance and skill. Hearing and vision, often adversely affected by the aging process, encourage increased isolation of the afflicted individual. Fears of ill health, chronic invalidism and death often contribute to mental illnesses and may contribute significantly to the many psychosomatic ailments of which the medical profession is becoming increasingly aware.

Decreased metabolic efficiency of the older person makes it difficult to keep warm; decreased ability to masticate food makes watchful care over the diet more important than earlier in life; decreased physical strength and vigor undermines energy and contributes to short-windedness and to other limitations upon physical exertion.

Since all the physiological changes of older people affect the pattern of living of the individuals involved, it is often necessary to work out new patterns of adjustment. All of them influence the type of work the church can do on behalf of the older person.

ECONOMIC PROBLEMS

Only brief investigation of the incomes of older people is needed to bring one to a realization that many older people in the United States have serious economic problems. In 1950, for instance, the median (middle) income of families in which the family head was aged sixty-five or over was only $1,903, as contrasted to a median income for all families of $3,319. The average (median) income of unrelated individuals (persons living alone or in households with no relative present) in the same year was $646 for persons past their sixty-fifth birthdays and $1,045 for persons of all age groups. One out of every seven families with family heads aged sixty-five and over and two out of every five aged individuals living alone or with non-relatives had incomes of less than $500. These figures include all money incomes received from wages or salary, net earnings from self-employment, interest, dividends, rents, social insurance and related programs, public assistance and contributions. They do not include money receipts from bank deposit withdrawals, tax refunds, gifts, lump-sum inheritances or insurance payments and income derived from the sale of assets.[10] Even though these amounts may be supplemented by income in kind gained from home-grown food, free housing and contributions of food and clothing, it is obvious that numerous senior citizens in the U. S. are seriously handicapped economically.

Reduced income often reduces social contacts at a time in life when these are needed more than for several earlier decades of life. It often limits the medical care sought by those who are most in need of it. It often leads to deficient diets and a form of malnutrition, as well as to housing in dwellings unfit for human habitation.

Since 1890 the proportion of men aged sixty-five and over who are in the labor force has decreased from over two out of three (68.2 per cent) to less than one out of three (32.4 per cent in 1959). The proportion of working women in the same age group decreased until 1940 (to 6.8 per cent from 7.6 per cent in 1890) and in the following decades increased to almost one out of ten (9.1 per cent in 1959).[11] This may indicate that older women are increasingly compelled to seek work outside the home or that they are receiving somewhat better treatment when they seek jobs, while men are increasingly forced to retire from the labor force because of old age.

With the increasing emphasis upon mechanization in farming and other occupations, the tendency is to place a premium upon certain characteristics and capacities of workers; this often operates to the detriment of the older worker. Recent developments in job-breakdown and specialization have resulted in a relative growth of the number of semi-skilled workers and a decline in the number of skilled workers. This has made it more difficult for older workers to retain prominent positions in the labor force. Mechanization has made it pos-

10. Committee on Aging and Geriatrics, *op. cit.*, pp. 49-50. See also Bureau of Labor Statistics, U. S. Department of Labor, *Employment and Economic Status of Older Men and Women* (Bulletin No. 1092), U. S. Government Printing Office, May, 1952. In 1958 almost 60 per cent of *all* aged persons had less than $1,000 money income, and another 20 per cent were in the $1,000 to $2,000 range. (*The Aged and Aging in the United States: A National Problem.* U.S. Government Printing Office, Senate Report No. 1121, 86th Congress, 2d Session, 1960.)

11. *The Aged and Aging, ibid.,* p. 28.

sible to hire unskilled or semi-skilled workers to do the work formerly done by skilled workers, many of whom have been of an older generation trained specifically for certain narrow types of work. The increasing speed of industrial processes also handicaps the older worker, while rapid technological changes make it impossible for most workers to use the same skills throughout their working lives.[12]

With the increasing automation of industry and business, many jobs and occupations are declining, and some are even disappearing. Older workers often are less flexible and adaptable and have a shorter working span remaining to them, so they often become unemployed as younger workers are trained for the new positions created by this trend.[13]

Most older people do not wish to retire as long as they are able, physically and mentally, to work. Yet compulsory retirement policies in many places of employment lay many people on the shelf prematurely. Private pensions, old age and survivor's insurance, old age assistance and savings provide their main sources of income after retirement. As we have already seen, that income is, for large numbers of them, insufficient to meet the demands of the American standard of living. Because of the puritan tradition of work for its own sake and of personal independence, and because home conditions have changed from what they were a century ago, retirement is often a major disintegrating factor for the older person.[14]

The housing facilities in which the aged are compelled by economic pressures to live are often unsuitable for them. Stairways to climb to bedroom or bathroom, large areas to keep clean and in order, kitchen facilities that require much stooping and stretching for use, and other undesirable features create serious problems for thousands of the aged. In addition, serious inadequacies of plumbing, heating, and electricity are found in many sub-standard dwellings occupied by older people

12. William H. Stead, "Trends of Employment in Relation to the Problems of the Aging," *Journal of Gerontology*, 4:290-297, Oct., 1949.

13. George Thomas, "Mechanized Industry Presents New Employment Hazards for Our Increasing Older Population," *The Railway Clerk*, Vol. 53, No. 23, p. 8, Dec. 1, 1954.

14. Michael T. Wermel and Selma Gelbaum, "Work and Retirement in Old Age," *American Journal of Sociology*, 51:16-21, July, 1945. A good discussion of the pros and cons of a fixed retirement age is found in four articles in *Annals of the American Academy of Political and Social Science*, 279:72-83, Jan., 1952.

because they are the only facilities available within their limited economic means.[15]

Faced with disappointment and disillusionment at reaching the "harvest years," finding the "golden years" to be a period of relative poverty, feeling themselves to be on the shelf and not permitted to make the contributions they still are able to make to the economic life of our nation, frustrated with the reduction of income which usually comes with retirement, and living in unpleasant, inconvenient, and unhealthful dwellings, it is no wonder that so many older persons are seriously maladjusted. The church has a tremendous challenge to face in the problems related to the economic plight of so many of our older citizens.

PROBLEMS OF SOCIAL RELATIONSHIPS

Since many older people do not know "their place" in society, it is no wonder that they cannot fill it. "The core of the aging problem . . . derives from the fact that . . . we have thus far failed to provide meaningful roles and opportunities for many of the millions who are living beyond the commonly accepted period of usefulness and into the new later years. . . . We must help these older people to help themselves — to better employ the skills, the experiences and the resources they have gained over a lifetime.

"In other words, we seek to foster a social environment in which the growing number of men and women who have passed the meridian of life may enjoy the greatest possible measure of good health, self realization and independence throughout their later years, and in which their productive capacities can be utilized to strengthen both our community and national well-being."[16]

The older individual is compelled to make choices, but he has no assurance that he has chosen "correctly" because there are no definite patterns of behavior laid down for him. When his actions involve other people, he must assume certain anticipated reciprocal behavior by them. When the expected behavior is not forthcoming, there often is disappointment. He

15. For a discussion of problems of housing older people see the report of the Committee on the Hygiene of Housing, *Housing an Aging Population,* American Public Health Association, 1953.

16. Committee on Aging, U. S. Department of Health, Education, and Welfare, *Aging — A Community Responsibility and Opportunity,* U. S. Government Printing Office, 1955, p. 2.

has no definite place in the contemporary social structure as elders in most preliterate societies have. He tends to become isolated from the occupational world when he is forced to retire from his work and isolated from social affairs because he is in a small conjugal family as contrasted to the large kinship groups of many other cultures. This social isolation may be a major source of senility and of the lack of personal adjustment of so many persons who are not mentally ill.[17]

There are many conditions in America which rob the aged of definite responsibilities. Without responsibilities they have a feeling of being useless and unwanted, of having lost a distinct place of respect and prestige. One of these conditions is the temporary nature of the typical American family. The family lasts from marriage until death (or in a minority of cases desertion or divorce) separates the couple. Years before that time the children typically have left to establish their own homes. In contrast, the older traditional type of rural family tended to outlive its members because it included three or more generations of people!

A major problem for many older persons is that of adjusting to the death of the spouse. More than half of all American women aged 65 and over, and more than two-thirds of those past the seventy-fifth birthday are widowed. This compares to just under one-fifth and one-third, respectively, of the men at corresponding ages. (The latter two figures are lower because men on the average marry women younger than themselves, die at a younger age, and are more likely to remarry after widowhood.) The man who becomes a widower may have to learn how to cook, keep house, keep his own clothes in order and care for many other details new to him. In addition, he will have to face the major problem of learning how to live alone. More often, however, this is a woman's problem. She

---

17. For a more complete discussion of this problem see Ralph Linton, "Concepts of Role and Status," in Theodore M. Newcomb and Eugene L. Hartley (eds.), *Readings in Social Psychology,* Henry Holt and Co., 1947, pp. 367-370; Ralph Linton, "Age and Sex Categories," *American Sociological Review,* 7:589-603, Oct., 1942; Talcott Parsons, "Age and Sex in the Social Structure of the United States," *ibid.,* pp. 604-616; Leo W. Simmons, *The Role of the Aged in Primitive Society,* Yale University Press, 1945; Leo W. Simmons, "Attitudes Toward Aging and the Aged: Primitive Societies," *Journal of Gerontology,* 1:72-95, Jan., 1946; Elaine Cumming *et al.,* "Disengagement — A Tentative Theory of Aging," *Sociometry,* 23:23-35, Mar. 1960, and Raymond Payne, "Some Theoretical Approaches to the Sociology of Aging," *Social Forces,* 38:359-362, May 1960.

may be forced to move to a smaller home, learn about business matters, economize severely because of reduced income and reconcile herself to living alone.

The aged have many problems associated with their friendships. The older person's friends often die before him; so the very persons who could do the most to bolster his morale may be beyond the place of help.

This type of problem is accentuated when mobility is great, as it is in our nation today. The old friends not only depart by death; they also move away. The older person himself may move away to some distant place where he must make new friends — if he is to have any friends at all. Older people who remain in the home community are left socially isolated in all too many instances as newcomers fill the occupational, social and residential gaps vacated by those who have departed.

Compulsory retirement is often a complete and sudden shock even when it is expected. This makes the individual feel unwanted and gives him the feeling that he is living as a parasite on the efforts and energy expended by others. One day a man works his eight hours; the next he is "on the shelf" for the rest of his life just because he has reached his sixty-fifth birthday. If he has no religion and no hobby or other avocation, he will face serious problems in the use of his time.

If the older citizen turns to civic affairs or to increased activity in social organizations to which he belongs, he may sense the need for major changes and desirable reforms in traditional practices. In all too many instances, however, the suggestions he makes will not be evaluated fairly by others, for the immediate impression of all too many people is that aged persons are "old fogies" whose suggested reforms would only take the nation back half a century or more.

The stereotype of old people also contributes to their problems. There is the idea that all of them have certain definite characteristics. This idea usually emphasizes the undesirable traits found in a few individuals. They thus are looked upon as living in the past, hopeful of getting back into the pleasant circumstances of an age gone by but forgetting the many unpleasant conditions of that same age. They are considered to be past the age of usefulness — except when a babysitter is needed! — and they are thought to desire only a final period of life at ease in the rocking chair.

Problems of social relationships are similarly increased by the tendency to emphasize individual accomplishment and individual competition to such an extent that the aged are sometimes actively competing with younger adults for recognition. With our emphasis upon speed, vigor, youthful beauty and similar values, older people usually lose out in the competition.

These problems reflect the basic characteristics of our society. To remove the problems it would be necessary to make wholesale changes in our culture that are entirely out of the question. These changes would include the complete overhaul of our family pattern, modification of retirement policies in places of employment, discontinuation of the mobility of our population, departure in whole or in part from our competitive economic and social order, decreased emphasis upon the person as an individual, return to a rural type of community life in which relationships in all social institutions and organizations closely coincide and overlap, decreased freedom of individuals to live as they please and an accompanying increased insistence that the various age groups play distinct roles in everyday living, and increased importance of government in many areas of life which are now considered to be purely "private."

It is probable that no one would want all the changes that would be necessary, if it were possible to spell them all out in detail, to remove the problem conditions of the aged. Desirable changes would undoubtedly include modification of cultural values and institutional practices to give older people a more satisfactory place in society and to help them continue living wholesome, productive lives that are beneficial to themselves and others. The church can contribute significantly to such changes.

EMOTIONAL AND MENTAL PROBLEMS[18]

A high prevalence of mental illness among the aged and a large number of border-line mental conditions are both a result of the previously discussed problems and a partial cause of some of them. Worrying that one's partner may become ill or die, fear of the possibilities of prolonged physical illness or disability, anxiety about financial problems, a sense of worthlessness at not contributing anything recognized as worthwhile to society, and feelings of disgrace because of dependence upon

18. Much of the material in this section was suggested by Robert J. Havighurst, "Social and Psychological Needs of the Aging," *Annals of the American Academy of Political and Social Science,* 279:11-17, Jan., 1952.

others for a livelihood contribute to many of the emotional ailments of older people.

Laid on the shelf occupationally, a man may daydream about the past until he reconstructs it into a much more flattering picture than he ever actually experienced. No longer able to perform the deeds which will bring him recognition, he may spin long tales of yesterday's exploits to those who will listen sympathetically.

Fantasies often serve as escape mechanisms. The present is uncomfortable and the future offers little, so it is natural for the senior adult to dwell upon his past pleasures and triumphs. If the reality of the past was not rosy enough, he can add color by exaggerating the favorable details. Thus the retired businessman who was always in actual life on the verge of bankruptcy may talk about his large and prosperous business, and the mother of disobedient and unruly children may tell during her senescence how well-behaved her little "angels" were when they were children. Giving advice is usually associated with this practice.

Some older persons regress to infancy and actually experience a second childhood to gain much-desired attention; they thus escape emotionally from the stark realities of life. This is manifested in various ways; it sometimes reaches such extreme forms as dependence upon others for feeding and dressing, or complete retirement to bed "because of illness" so that others will wait upon them.

The loss of hearing, sight, or memory that is characteristic of so many older persons similarly is often not due solely to the actual degeneration of bodily faculties. The older individual is sometimes hard of hearing except when others talk about him, forgetful of unpleasant appointments he has found it necessary to make but not of the pleasant ones, and he is in other ways psychosomatically afflicted.

Another common escape mechanism is found in the hallucinations of some aged persons. They may speak to absent persons or to loved ones long since departed from this life, or they may engage in other forms of deviant behavior. When adults do this, we become alarmed; but when small children do the very same thing, we praise them as being "cute" or as having exceptionally good imaginations.

The self-confidence of aged and middle-aged persons is daily undermined by attitudes of others toward them that they are too old to do useful work, too old to make their own decisions, too old to learn new ways, too old to go out alone.[19] It is no wonder that these adverse influences seriously injure the aged and middle-aged.

The memory of many older persons for distant events is sharp, but the memory for yesterday is obscure and distorted. The humiliation of today's events may obliterate recollection of the depressing and debasing occurrences of these later years of life and make one live in the past — a past that is naturally reconstructed into an even more successful and happy memory than it actually was, for the mind tends to select the pleasant events and magnify them while it gradually drops the unpleasant and painful ones.

Resenting segregation and isolation from social and economic activities in which he has previously played an active part, the senior citizen may be filled with indignation that leads him to become defiant and to spurn the very acts of kindness that are shown him in his need. Many of the ill manners and disgusting actions of certain older persons may be a result of an inward attitude of hopelessness and futility that is transferred to the outward circumstances in which they find themselves. Old resentments, anxieties and hatreds are easily magnified when one is no longer busy, when one is alone, and when one feels he is no longer needed.

"The past is ever with us." Sometimes in old age, when the past is at its maximum for an individual, there is a tendency for the past to dominate and to fill him with persistent feelings of resentment, anxiety, and insecurity. With confidence in himself so shaken that he may no longer feel competent economically, physically, socially and personality-wise, the individual may become so severely maladjusted as even to need institutional treatment for his senility. Filled with despondency and dismay in the present, he also may fear the gradual approach of death, or he may long for death and even attempt to commit suicide in self-directed efforts to solve his problems.

The many shocks suffered by the normal older person are crises greater than those that face the average person at any other period of life. Death of the spouse, loss of a job and inability to secure a new one, the onset of incurable physical disorders, and the realization that one is old or is being treated as old may make the older person forget that he has a future both before and after death and may contribute to mental

19. Helen Hardy Brunot, *Old Age in New York City*, Welfare Council of New York City, 1943, p. 14.

illnesses of varying degrees of severity and thus to an accentuation of the various other problems faced. In the emotional and mental problems of old age lies a distinct challenge for the church.

SPIRITUAL PROBLEMS

There is a sense in which every problem of an individual is a spiritual problem, or at least has spiritual implications. Among the other problems of older people, however, are some that are much more clearly of a spiritual and religious nature than others.

One of these is fear of the future, especially of death, that often torments the conscious or the subconscious mind of the person who cannot but realize that he is nearing the grave. The comfort and hope imparted through religion can be a major source of alleviation of this dread.

When other problem conditions interfere, it is often difficult to get to church to engage in public worship and in fellowship with others of like faith. In the winter in cold climates the heating and ventilation of the church facilities may be poor and very uncomfortable to the older person. High steps at the church entrance, heavy and ominous doors that frighten the stranger away, and other physical obstacles discourage many older people from attending. The lack of suitable transportation facilities, the cost of paying membership dues or of contributing through a sense of obligation to voluntary offerings, poor eyesight, poor hearing, poor acoustics in the building, careless enunciation and diction by the preacher and other speakers, and other difficulties both within the church and within the older person himself contribute to infrequent attendance and a low level of general participation in the church by many older people.

Not only the religious group activities of the older person, but also many of his own personal acts of devotion to God often suffer. Because of poor eyesight and small print, it becomes difficult for many to read their Bibles and devotional literature. Because of poor hearing, they may miss religious radio and television broadcasts that otherwise could impart spiritual help to them. The impairment of their senses may also limit the benefits received from visits of church groups and from the various services provided by the clergy.

Many older persons carry with them a burden of guilt that sends them prematurely to the grave. They sometimes have a sense of failure and regret for not having attained goals set early in life. Some of them have violated the customs (folkways and mores) of society either privately or publicly, and others have engaged in activities definitely classified as sinful both in religious and in social circles. Their guilty consciences may result from truly despicable activities, or they may result from misconceived notions of moral and ethical standards. Regardless of the nature or the source of such feelings of guilt, they create tensions and mental problems that are not easily resolved.

More directly than in the other anomalous conditions of the aged, the church has a significant task to perform in solving the spiritual problems and lifting the spiritual burdens of older persons.

THE NEGLECT OF THE AGED

In spite of the numerous problems they are prone to face, widespread attention to older people and their needs has emerged only in the past ten or fifteen years. The early tendency was neither to revere nor to reject old age, but to ignore it in the supposition that it is only a state of mind which can be eliminated if one keeps busy — i.e., if one acts youthful.[20]

The neglect of the aged has been seen, in the past especially, among those who are concerned with the psychological well-being or mental health of our population,[21] among sociologists,[22] in the medical profession,[23] by the public in gen-

20. Robert J. Havighurst, "Old Age — An American Problem," op. cit., pp. 298-304.

21. George Lawton, "A Long-Range Research Program in the Psychology of Old Age and Aging," Journal of Social Psychology, 12:101-114, Aug., 1940.

22. Belle Boon Beard's analysis of the tables of contents and indices of twenty sociology books on the family showed that eight had no reference whatever to the aged, and only two treated the subject comprehensively. A total of fifty pages out of 10,697 were devoted to old people in these books. ("Are the Aged Ex-Family?" Social Forces, 27:274-279, Mar., 1949.) More recent books usually include data on the aged.

23. Medical neglect of the speciality of geriatrics has been due in part to the lack of a spectacular element in that type of work, and in part to the fact that it is not as remunerative a specialty as some other branches of medicine, the fact that the physician's efforts ultimately must end in failure with the death of his patient, and the great demand for original observation and research by the specialist because so little has been written about it until recently. (This pattern has begun to change in recent years.) Cf. Malford W. Thewlis, The Care of the Aged (Geriatrics), C. V. Mosby Co., third edition, 1941, pp. 25f.

eral,[24] and even by the church and the clergy.[25]

The neglect of the aged has been due partly to ignorance of the problem conditions of older people and of the scope of the problem. We have suddenly realized that there are millions of aged in our country who are often economically dependent, physically impaired, mentally depressed or socially isolated. Only as we have awakened to this realization have we begun to take action.

A second reason for the neglect of the aged has been the disagreeableness of the stereotype of the older person. We often find persons who are repulsive and who fail to arouse our sympathy because of their peevishness, selfishness, offensive actions, disagreeable odors and suspicious attitudes,[26] but we tend to forget that there are countless others, perhaps a majority of them, who have very few if any of these unattractive characteristics.

This neglect is also due to the psychological barriers that tend to erect themselves between the generations. Children tend to stand aloof from the parental generation, for their interests frequently are not the same as those of their parents. This tends to carry through to a neglect of the generation that is older than one's own, or sometimes to a tendency to treat the oldsters as they treated us when we were children. "After all, are not all aged people in their second childhood?" tends to be the reasoning that undergirds this practice. Some actually try to "get even with" their elders for abuses or imagined abuses suffered through them during the process of growing up.

A fourth source of neglect of older people on the part of many is the fear of their own approaching later maturity.

24. Although Edward J. Stieglitz wrote these words almost two decades ago, they hold true today to a great extent: "Society as a whole looks upon aging as either a catastrophe or a sin. Respect for mature years has been on the wane. This attitude creates a severe and at least partially unjustified handicap to the aging." (Chapter XVII in Oscar J. Kaplan (ed.), *Mental Disorders in Later Life,* Stanford University Press, 1945, p. 423.)

25. See Paul B. Maves and J. Lennart Cedarleaf, *Older People and the Church,* Abingdon-Cokesbury Press, 1949, pp. 27-29. As recently as 1960 Henry Jacobson stated that the older person is beginning to receive the attention he deserves from government, industry, and everyone except the Christian church. ("The Problem of the Senior Citizen," *Eternity,* Vol. 11, No. 10, pp. 22-24, 39-40, Oct., 1960.)

26. See Malford W. Thewlis, *op. cit.,* p. 24, for a discussion of some of these traits.

Some fear the time when they can expect to manifest some of the characteristics of the aged and to suffer some of the abuses of old age. Whether one is a medical doctor, social worker, clergyman, or other professional worker or a citizen who has older friends, relatives, and acquaintances, a subconscious desire to avoid thinking about one's own later maturity can lead him to avoid association with them because of the painful reminders this association sends to the unconscious mind.

Mistaken ideas that people have about the aged and their needs are a fifth source of their neglect. There is a tendency to think that all they want is financial security and freedom from responsibility, when in reality they want a feeling of being useful, being loved, being wanted. Sometimes it is assumed that the economic distress many of them experience is a result of their own carelessness and improvidence. However, millions of older people in the United States have lived on a hand-to-mouth basis because of their position in the labor force; we cannot condemn them for not saving that which they never received.

By over-emphasis in our churches and other community organizations upon children and youth, we have cultivated the attitude that time spent with older people is wasted. The idea is expressed openly by some that if we spend time with the aged and help to meet their needs, we will soon have no congregations left. Others believe, mistakenly, that the aged cannot be changed; why spend time trying to convert them to Christianity or trying to develop Christian graces and wholesome personalities when it is impossible to do so? Other similar notions reflecting general ignorance about old people have stood in the way of improving their condition and have encouraged many people to avoid, neglect or ignore them in our society.[27]

A sixth source, perhaps the most significant, of the neglect of the aged is the set of values that underlies life in America. Great emphasis is placed upon that which is new and upon

27. Even graduate students in a leading teachers college have been found to accept many stereotypes and misconceptions about older people. See Jacob Tuckman and Irving Lorge, "Attitudes Towards Old People," *Journal of Social Psychology*, 37:249-260, May, 1953. Cf. Seymour Axelrod and Carl Eisdorfer, "Attitudes Toward Old People: An Empirical Analysis of the Stimulus-Group Validity of the Tuckman-Lorge Questionnaire," *Journal of Gerontology*, 16:75-80, Jan., 1961.

those who are young in our relatively youthful and rapidly changing nation. We are encouraged to turn in last year's automobile or refrigerator for this year's model; and we are almost daily confronted with billboard and newspaper pictures, movies, radio and television programs, contests, and festivals that glorify youth and tend to identify all beauty with that which is new and young. This exaggerated premium on youth in American culture often has a calamitous effect on the mental health of the aging.[28]

Economic aggressiveness and the desire "to get ahead" tend to make Americans think that unless they are advancing economically and socially, climbing ever higher on the ladder of success, they are old and hence no longer useful. Whenever signs of diminishing economic competitive ability begin to appear in the individual, whenever he cannot fit in with the increasing efficiency, mass production, and automation of industry and business, and whenever he has lost the superficial signs of outward physical "beauty," he is relegated to the scrap heap of old age.[29]

CONCLUSION

The President's Commission on the Health Needs of the Nation stated in its report to President Truman that all areas of the lives of older persons are inextricably interrelated:

> Unfortunately, older persons today live in a society that is in many ways becoming uncongenial and unfavorable to them. Encountering adverse attitudes, older people tend to lose their dignity and their sense of worth. Their role in the family, if one remains to them, is not conducive to self-respect; opportunities for gainful employment are denied them on the basis of their calendar years; fewer and fewer opportunities for self-maintenance remain in a social order which still regards self-maintenance as the only respectable way to live; dependency, total or partial, is forced upon almost two-thirds of the older generations through no fault of their own.

> As the health and social needs of aging persons become more numerous, too often their own means to satisfy them either diminish or are entirely lacking. Dental treatment and dentures, hear-

28. Maurice E. Linden, "Effects of Social Attitudes on the Mental Health of the Aging," *Geriatrics,* 12:109-114, 1957.
29. Cf. Eduard C. Lindeman, "The Sociological Challenge of the Aging Population," in Proceedings of the Eastern States Health Education Conference, Mar. 31-Apr. 1, 1949, *The Social and Biological Challenge of Our Aging Population,* Columbia University Press, 1950, pp. 171-183.

ing aids, eyeglasses, and other devices to help them to function more effectively are hard to get; housing, which should be more adequate, tends to be much less so; leisure, of which they have previously had very little and of which they now have a super-abundance, easily becomes a source of boredom and may lead to withdrawal from life. This generalized description may appear exaggerated; certainly it does not appear to every older person.

The real point is that disease and disability in old people are inextricably bound up with their total situation — their social arrangements, their physical and mental fitness, their economic and occupational adequacy, their spiritual status. It is impossible to treat sick older people adequately without considering every area of their lives.[30]

It is because of these facts that old age is a social problem. Old age in and of itself is not a social problem, for it is natural and inevitable. Sickness and physical disability are found in every age group. The natural concomitants of aging certainly contribute to the problems of the older person, but why should anyone set old people apart as a special age group and discriminate against them all? Instead, would it not be more consistent with democratic as well as Christian ideology to consider each older person as a *person* in the light of his own needs, interests, abilities and surroundings? It is primarily the reactions of people toward aging and the conditions that surround the aged that create problems for them.[31]

Confronted with all the problems which our society contributes to older people, the elderly individual is often more open to the message of the church than he has ever been before. The remainder of this book is devoted to the contributions religion, and especialy organized religion or the church, can and does make to him and to the prevention, alleviation and solution of his problems. Its negative influence also receives due attention, for this is not a one-sided account attempting to vindicate the church as a social institution.

30. President's Commission on the Health Needs of the Nation, *op. cit.*, vol. II, p. 92.

31. Cf. George Lawton, *Aging Successfully*, Columbia University Press, 1946, pp. 167f., and Edward B. Allen, "Psychological Factors That Have a Bearing on the Aging Process," in Proceedings of the Eastern States Health Education Conference, *op. cit.*, pp. 116f.

CHAPTER 3

THE RELIGION OF OLDER PEOPLE

BECAUSE OF THE NUMEROUS PROBLEMS older people experience in our society, because of the gradual approach of death, because they have more time to think than they have had for decades previously, and for various other reasons, many older people turn to religion in old age with renewed fervor.

As psychologist George Lawton has indicated, the longer we live, the greater the number of past experiences we have had upon which to reflect, the greater our search to understand the meaning of joy and suffering, the greater our hunger to explain our lives to ourselves, and the greater our desire to seek justification for the world and for human nature as we have found them. The result is a declining interest in material aspects of life. This takes place largely, to be sure, as a result of reduced ability to take part in them, but also as a result of the piling up of knowledge and experience. With the declining interest in material things comes a growing concern in things spiritual.[1]

It is natural for older people to turn to the church. Usually it is more accessible than other agencies and institutions in the community. It is often the only service agency known to many persons, and many older people have grown up in the church and have various ties with it. As they grow older, many people find that religion means more to them than it did in the past; religious activities, therefore, do not decline as much with disabilities in old age as do activities in some other areas.[2]

1. George Lawton, *Aging Successfully*, Columbia University Press, 1946, pp. 167-168.
2. Paul B. Maves and J. Lennart Cedarleaf, *Older People and the Church*, Abingdon-Cokesbury Press, 1949, p. 31, and Frances C. Jeffers and Claude R. Nichols, "The Relationship of Activities and Attitudes to Physical Well-Being in Older People," *Journal of Gerontology*, 16:67-70, Jan., 1961.

On the other hand, with curtailed income, those who are sensitive to such social conventions as not attending without contributing or as wearing "Sunday best" clothing to church are often reluctant to continue their church fellowship when they can make little or no financial contribution or when they are without what they consider to be suitable clothing. It takes great effort for many older persons to dress up and prepare for church, to say nothing of getting to the church building, up the flight of stairs that is a barrier to most of them, and into pews where acoustics may be so poor that they can hear but little of the service with their declining sense of hearing. These influences might be expected to counteract the others and to encourage many older people to drop at least the overt activity of church attendance.

RELIGIOUS ACTIVITIES AND BELIEFS OF OLDER PEOPLE

What do we know about the actual religious behavior and beliefs of the aged in the United States? Various surveys and studies give us some information from which we may be able to reach conclusions about the relative religiosity of older people.

A study by Selz Mayo led to certain findings about the participation of older people in rural areas of Wake County, North Carolina, in organized community activities. Mayo found that the peak of intensity of social participation for these rural people comes at the age period fifty-five to fifty-nine with a sharp drop at later ages. Four fifths of their social participation in organized activities was in religious activities, and generally the higher participation scores of some individuals resulted from more intense participation in a few religious activities. Six-tenths of the population aged sixty and over participated only in church and church auxiliary organizations, and only about one out of ten did not participate at all in religious organizations. For every one hundred older persons there were 149 memberships in religious organizations and only thirty-eight memberships in all other types of organizations.[3] The dominance of the church and its auxiliary organizations in the social participation of older people in rural areas

3. Selz C. Mayo, "Social Participation Among the Older Population in Rural Areas of Wake County, North Carolina," *Social Forces*, 30:53-59, Oct., 1951.

of this North Carolina county is probably characteristic of many other rural areas in the United States, particularly in the South.

Similar findings have emerged from studies of many urban areas as well. Webber's field survey in 1951 of the organized social life of 474 randomly selected retired persons in the cities of West Palm Beach and Orlando, Florida, revealed that more than half of the 101 organizations in which these persons reported participation were churches or church-related groups. In the Orlando sample of retired persons about half the local memberships were in churches with an additional ten per cent in church-affiliated associations, such as Bible classes, men's clubs, Sunday schools, ladies' aids, guilds, and missionary societies. Religious services were attended much more often than meetings of secular organizations, although about one-fourth of the subjects never attended religious services. Men attended less than women, and attendance was found to decline as age increased. Similar patterns of church attendance were found in the West Palm Beach sample, except that they did not attend as regularly.[4]

Another study indicated that sixty-nine per cent of the responding people who had migrated away from their home communities and were living in a trailer park in Florida reported having attended church in the original home community, but after immigration only fifty-nine per cent attended church. The average number of times the attenders went to church per month was not significantly changed by migration to Florida (3.4 times per month in the home community, and 3.6 times in Florida).[5]

In "Prairie City," a small midwestern city which researchers from the University of Chicago have studied over a period of years, it was discovered that only two per cent of the people over the age of sixty-five have active participation in the church with responsibility as church officer, committee member, Sunday-school teacher, etc.; sixty-one per cent have frequent and active participation in religious activities with no responsibility; fifteen per cent have passive interest, seldom

4. Irving L. Webber, "The Organized Social Life of the Retired: Two Florida Communities," *American Journal of Sociology*, 59:340-346, Jan., 1954.
5. G. C. Hoyt, "The Life of the Retired in a Trailer Park," *American Journal of Sociology*, 59:361-370, Jan., 1954.

attending church though perhaps listening to sermons on the radio; eighteen per cent have no church affiliation and no attendance; and only four per cent reject religion and the church.[6]

Havighurst and Albrecht conclude that there is no evidence in Prairie City of a large-scale "turning to religion" as people grow older. Most of them continue the religious habits of their middle years, although it is customary for them to drop out of leadership positions in the churches gradually after they reach the age of sixty. Older men drop out of church activity more rapidly than women, probably because their activities in the church are more apt to involve administrative and teaching positions which are passed down to a younger generation, while women are occupied in women's organizations and find themselves in demand for sewing, quilting, serving at church dinners, and other church projects. Hence older women generally are of more use in the church than older men and therefore get more out of church life.[7] Numerous studies have shown that women participate more than men in religious organizations and activities in old age as well as in the younger periods of life.

Old people attend church in about the same proportions as the middle aged. One suspects that a larger proportion of them is hindered by physical disabilities, so the same overall attendance rates may represent actual increases in attendance among those who are physically able to attend. Older people are more likely than other adults to have an image of themselves as being religious and to say that they believe in life after death.[8] Churches are important to a substantial proportion of the population in such retirement communities as St. Cloud, Florida. More of its churches are fundamentalist than

6. Robert J. Havighurst and Ruth Albrecht, *Older People*, Longmans, Green and Co., 1953, pp. 201f.

7. *Ibid.*, p. 203, and Ruth E. Albrecht, "The Meaning of Religion to Older People — The Social Aspect," in Delton L. Scudder, editor, *Organized Religion and the Older Person*, University of Florida Press, 1958, pp. 53-70.

8. Milton L. Barron, "The Role of Religion and Religious Institutions in Creating the Milieu of Older People," in Delton L. Scudder, *op. cit.*, pp. 12-33. (Barron's conclusions are based upon nation-wide and New York City surveys.) See also Philip Taietz and Olaf F. Larson, "Social Participation and Old Age," *Rural Sociology*, 21:229-238, Sept.-Dec., 1956.

is usual in peninsular Florida; one-third of them are evangelical and "sectarian."[9]

A thorough survey of people aged sixty-five years and over in one section of Chicago found that 35.6 per cent experienced difficulty attending church, yet over seventy per cent of the predominantly Catholic sample reported monthly or more frequent church attendance. Over half believed that religion had become more helpful to them during the preceding ten years. Sixty per cent had not received a pastoral visit by a clergyman, but only six per cent saw such visiting as a means by which the church could help them. Women were more active in church attendance and Catholic religious practices than men, but the men were more likely than the women to have increased their church attendance since the age of sixty-five.[10]

Additional evidence of the religious behavior of the aged comes from various public opinion polls and surveys. An American Institute of Public Opinion poll in 1944 included the question, "Do you believe there is a life after death?" Of the respondents aged fifty years and over, seventy-nine per cent answered yes, ten per cent no, and eleven per cent were undecided or had no opinion. The corresponding responses for those aged twenty to twenty-nine years were seventy, seventeen, and thirteen per cent, respectively, and for those aged thirty to forty-nine years they were seventy-six, thirteen, and eleven per cent.[11] Is this an indication that the belief in immortality increases with age? At least in opinion polls during and since the 1940's the older generation was somewhat more likely to claim that belief than the younger generations.

A nation-wide survey of Americans aged eighteen and over was designed to study the religious beliefs and practices of persons from all parts of the nation and all nationalities, races and religions. The results were analyzed in terms of certain

9. Gordon J. Aldridge, "The Role of Older People in a Florida Retirement Community," *Geriatrics*, 11:223-226, May, 1956.

10. Charles T. O'Reilly and Margaret M. Pembroke, *Older People in a Chicago Community*, Research Report of the School of Social Work, Loyola University, n. d. (c. 1957), pp. 30-38, and Charles T. O'Reilly, "Religious Practice and Personal Adjustment," *Sociology and Social Research*, 42:119-121, Nov.-Dec., 1958. Comparable findings are reported in Charles T. O'Reilly and Margaret M. Pembroke, *OAA Profile*: *The Old Age Assistance Client in Chicago*, Loyola University Press, 1961, pp. 67-75.

11. Hadley Cantril (ed.), and Mildred Strunk (compiler), *Public Opinion, 1935-1946*, Princeton University Press, 1951, p. 310.

characteristics, one of which is age. Some of the pertinent findings were that older people are more certain that there is a God, do not attend church as frequently, are more serious about preparing for life after death than in trying to live comfortably (a pronounced contrast to the younger groups), and tend to read Scripture more than the young.[12]

No more concise summary of the pattern of religious activities of older people in the United States can be made than the following words of Ernest W. Burgess, a leading sociologist who is now devoting much of his time to research on the aged: "Older citizens increase their religious activities and dependence upon religion. Frequency of church attendance drops in the 80's and 90's. Incapacity to go to church, however, is more than compensated for by listening to church services over the radio and by Bible reading."[13]

EFFECTS OF RELIGION ON OLDER PEOPLE

How do the religious activities and beliefs of the aged affect them personally? Psychologist George Lawton has listed trust in God or "health of the spirit" as second only to good health as a source of contentment in later life. As a result of his counseling of older people, he placed it ahead of a cheerful state of mind, money, friends, gainful occupation, pleasant relationships with members of one's family, the satisfaction of doing things for others, and ordinary kindness and consideration from others.[14]

Similarly, sociologist Judson T. Landis found in a study of a random sample of 450 people aged sixty-five and over that the happiest old people are the ones who visit with friends often and attend church regularly. He does qualify his finding with the reservation that it is probably not so much that church-going makes one better adjusted as that church attend-

12. *Catholic Digest*, Vol. 17, No. 1, Nov., 1952, p. 4; No. 2, Dec., 1952, p. 5; No. 7, May, 1953, p. 80, and Vol. 18, No. 7, May, 1954, p. 24.

13. Ernest W. Burgess, "Family Living in the Later Decades," *Annals of the American Academy of Political and Social Science.* 279:107, Jan., 1952. Detroit Area Study data indicate that church attendance patterns are not significantly different from those of younger people, except that a larger proportion of the very old never attend church. (Harold L. Orbach, "Aging and Religion: Church Attendance in the Detroit Metropolitan Area," *Geriatrics*, 16:530-540, Oct., 1961.)

14. George Lawton, "Happiness in Old Age," *Mental Hygiene*, 27:231-237, Apr., 1943.

ance is an indication of a sociable nature: those who attend church also visit with friends often, belong to lodges and ladies' aids and are active in other organizations in the community.[15]

Among other characteristics related to "success in old age" among 349 successful and 204 problem cases of old people were church attendance and philosophy of life.[16] This correlation between church attendance, philosophy of life, and successful old age is an indication of a *possible* cause-and-effect relationship between religion and successful adjustment in old age. This possibility is also indicated by a series of studies that have been made with the help of *Your Activities and Attitudes,* an inventory prepared by Ernest W. Burgess, Ruth S. Cavan and Robert J. Havighurst to measure personal adjustment in old age.[17] The development of the two instruments in this inventory and their use with 499 men and 759 women is described in a work by social scientists at the University of Chicago.[18] They found that the degree of participation and the attitude toward participation in social activities decreased with age after the sixtieth birthday. Nevertheless, satisfaction with religion and the derivation of a feeling of security from it increased with age. The percentage of both men and women with favorable attitudes toward religion was found to increase with age. Belief in a life after death, which was accepted by most people in their sixties, was universally accepted by all in their nineties.

In a study of patterns of poor adjustment of older people in Akron and in Kansas City, Schmidt listed twenty factors associated with poor adjustment in both men and women. Among these were a lack of or infrequent church attendance

15. Judson T. Landis, "Hobbies and Happiness in Old Age," *Recreation,* 35:642, Jan., 1942.

16. S. L. Pressey and Elizabeth Simcoe, "Case Study Comparisons of Successful and Problem Old People," *Journal of Gerontology,* 5:168-175, Apr., 1950. Among persons successfully adjusted to retirement, 42 per cent were church members, but only 17 per cent of a contrasting group of unhappy, maladjusted retired persons were members. (Paul F. Verden and Archer L. Michael, "A Comparison of Successfully and Unsuccessfully Retired Groups," *Geriatrics,* 14:528-534, Aug., 1959.)

17. E. W. Burgess, R. S. Cavan and R. J. Havighurst, *Your Activities and Attitudes,* Science Research Associates, 1948.

18. Ruth S. Cavan, Ernest W. Burgess, Robert J. Havighurst and Herbert Goldhamer, *Personal Adjustment in Old Age,* Science Research Associates, 1949.

and less frequent church attendance in the present than in the past.[19]

Retired school teachers were studied by Joseph H. Britton. He discovered ten factors associated with good personal adjustment. Among these were church membership,. frequent reading of the Bible or prayer book and belief in an after life.[20] A comparable study of 161 retired YMCA secretaries revealed four chief areas associated with good personal adjustment in old age: health, religion, economic security and social mobility.[21]

Two studies of older people living in homes for the aged have resulted in similar conclusions. Pan's first study of 156 persons living in twelve institutions for the aged indicated that one of nine areas correlated with better adjustment in old age is that of religious faith and philosophy of life.[22] His more recent study of 730 aged members of 151 old people's homes under Protestant auspices indicated that among seventeen items associated with good personal adjustment were church attendance once a week or more and greater church attendance than ten years previously. He concluded that the six categories of attitudes associated significantly with good adjustment were health, family, leisure time, employment, usefulness and religion.[23]

Among thirty-one factors Mrs. Shanas found favorable to good adjustment among old age assistance recipients were church

19. John F. Schmidt, *Patterns of Poor Adjustment in Persons of Later Maturity*, Ph.D. Thesis, Department of Sociology, University of Chicago, 1950. See also "Patterns of Poor Adjustment in Old Age," *American Journal of Sociology*, 57:33-42, July, 1951.

20. Joseph H. Britton, *A Study of the Adjustment of Retired School Teachers*, Ph.D. Thesis, Committee on Human Development, University of Chicago, 1949. See also "A Study of the Adjustment of Retired School Teachers," *The American Psychologist*, 4:308, July, 1949.

21. Jean Oppenheimer Britton, *A Study of the Adjustment of Retired YMCA Secretaries*, Ph.D. Thesis, Committee on Human Development, University of Chicago, 1949.

22. Ju-Shu Pan, *A Study of the Personal and Social Adjustment of the Old People in the Homes for Aged*, M.A. Thesis, Department of Sociology, University of Chicago, 1947.

23. Ju-Shu Pan, *A Comparison of Factors in the Personal Adjustment of Old People in the Protestant Church Homes for the Aged and the Old People Living Outside of Institutions*, Ph.D. Thesis, Department of Sociology, University of Chicago, 1950. See also "Factors in Personal Adjustment of Old People in Protestant Homes for the Aged," *American Sociological Review*, 16:379-381, June, 1951, and "Social Adjustment of Aged People," *Sociology and Social Research*, 33:424-430, July-Aug., 1949.

attendance once a week or more, regular Bible reading, listening to radio church services once a week or more and belief in an after life. Her findings also verified the validity of the Burgess-Cavan-Havighurst attitudes inventory as a satisfactory scale for the measurement of personal adjustment in old age.[24]

A project that dealt directly with the church and the problems of old age was conducted by Paul B. Maves and J. Lennart Cedarleaf for the Department of Pastoral Services of the Federal Council of the Churches of Christ in America in cooperation with the New York Conference of the Methodist Church.[25] Cedarleaf found that a well-qualified and properly-trained minister who understood the problems of old age could do much to aid the older person to find and to maintain a sense of meaningfulness in life and to accept his role as an older person. Maves made an exploratory study of thirteen Protestant churches to learn about their programs for oldsters. He found that no special programs were planned for the aged in these churches and that the efforts that were being made for them were unconsciously falling into an exploitative pattern for the sake of the church, rather than being related to the needs and interests of the people. Yet the participation of older people in the church was on the whole better than that of any other adult group.[26]

Among the 292 old people interviewed in the "Back of the Yards" area of Chicago, only a slight, statistically insignificant relationship was found between feelings of loneliness and "less active" practice of religion; but happiness was significantly related to their frequency of church attendance, the "very happy" attending church more frequently than the others.[27] Fifty-seven per cent of the 140 retired Negroes located in an Orangeburg County, South Carolina, survey said the church and religion held more meaning for them since than before retirement, and 42.2 per cent said it held the same meaning. The church was in second place as a major hobby and activity for these older people, only gardening and farming ranking

24. Ethel Shanas, *The Personal Adjustment of Recipients of Old Age Assistance,* Ph.D. Thesis, Department of Sociology, University of Chicago, 1949.

25. P. B. Maves and J. L. Cedarleaf, *op. cit.,* and Paul B. Maves, *The Christian Religious Education of Older People,* Federal Council of the Churches of Christ in America, 1950.

26. *Ibid.*

27. Charles T. O'Reilly and Margaret M. Pembroke, *op. cit.,* pp. 35-36.

higher.   Preaching was ninth on the list of fourteen types of major hobbies and activities.[28]

An Austin, Texas, study of nursing home residents and persons aged sixty and over in the general population found the former group to be significantly more socially isolated and less well adjusted than the non-institutionalized residents of the community.   In both samples the persons who attended church once a month or more were more likely to have a high level of adjustment as measured by the Burgess-Cavan-Havighurst Attitudes Inventory than those who attended church less than once a month.   In addition, persons in the non-institutional sample who read the Bible once a week or oftener were more likely to have a high level of adjustment than those who reported reading the Bible less often.[29]

The impact of religious faith is clearly evident in attitudes toward sickness and death.   Patients who bring a Bible with them to the hospital and prominently display it often give the nurses, doctor, and hospital staff much trouble.   Their actions reflect insecurities which are absent in the stable, secure person who is active in civic and church life and who seldom brings a Bible with him to the hospital.   Anxieties of patients are sometimes accentuated by the unexpected visit of a minister just before an operation or during illness, so medical doctors, recognizing the close relationship between the emotions and physical healing, are discouraged by the visits of certain clergymen.   In addition, patients seldom speak with their medical doctor about religious matters.   After twenty-five years of practice, the Director of Kirkpatrick Memorial Institute of Physical Medicine and Rehabilitation in Winter Park, Florida, also stated, "I recall no person who called out to God or audibly prayed when he knew he was dying.   Usually, these persons are exerting every bit of energy in a struggle to keep alive."[30] He has observed, however, that when patients regain conscious-

28. R. Grann Lloyd, "Social and Personal Adjustment of Retired Persons," *Sociology and Social Research*, 39:312-316, May-June, 1955. Cf. the findings on satisfaction with religion and church activities reported in Mary W. Laurence, "Sources of Satisfaction in the Lives of Working Women," *Journal of Gerontology*, 16:163-167, April, 1961.

29. Frances Gillespie Scott, "Factors in the Personal Adjustment of Institutionalized and Non-Institutionalized Aged," *American Sociological Review*, 20:538-546, Oct., 1955.

30. Nila Kirkpatrick Covalt, "The Meaning of Religion to Older People," *Geriatrics*, 15:658-664, Sept., 1960.

ness after operations or a coma, they often give visions and thoughts similar to dreams a spiritual significance.

The attitudes toward death of religious persons are demonstrated by research to be significantly different from those of the non-religious. Although this may be due partly to traditional cultural definitions of death which include a religious interpretation of it, it also "seems logical to infer that the eschatologically oriented person contemplates death in a positive manner," for there is a statistically significant relationship between religiosity and attitudes toward death. Persons who engage in little religious activity tend in general to have fearful attitudes toward death. "Persons with more fundamental religious convictions and habits look forward to death more than do those with less fundamental convictions and less activity."[31]

As a result of the problems of old age, findings of studies like those reported in this chapter, and practical experiences of church leaders, numerous denominations, church congregations, and councils of churches consciously minister to the special needs of the aging.[32] One would expect their ministry to emphasize primarily spiritual needs of senior citizens, yet most official publications of major Protestant denominations on the subject stress social, economic, health and mental hygiene needs. A "social-service orientation" is more pronounced than the "personal religious-experience orientation" if the amount of attention given a topic in published materials is an adequate index of the emphasis placed on that topic in actual affairs.[33] Regardless of the chief focus of their attention, however, churches increasingly shoulder a specific responsibility of serving the aging population. The Protestant theological orientation that views all of life as sacred makes a church ministry to educational,

---

31. Wendell M. Swenson, "Attitudes Toward Death in an Aged Population," *Journal of Gerontology*, 16:49-52, Jan., 1961 (quotations from pp. 51 and 52). Similar findings are reported by Frances C. Jeffers, Claude R. Nichols, and Carl Eisdorfer, "Attitudes of Older Persons Toward Death: A Preliminary Study," *ibid.*, pp. 53-56.

32. The many and varied types of services provided by churches and synagogues for aging people are described in a 38-page summary, *Background Paper on Services of Religious Groups for the Aging*, prepared under direction of the National Advisory Committee for the White House Conference on Aging, U.S. Government Printing Office, Nov., 1960.

33. Leonard Z. Breen and Carol Trumpe, "Religious Groups and Conceptions of Aging," Abstract of Paper Presented at the 14th Annual Meeting of the Gerontological Society, *Journal of Gerontology*, 16:400, Oct., 1961.

housing, social service, mental health, and other needs just as much a "spiritual" service as traditional church functions whenever sacred attitudes and motivations are stressed.

CONCLUSION

The studies reported in this chapter have agreed in the finding that religion is significantly related to various indicators of the personal adjustment of old people. For the most part, however, they were not directly focussed upon the subject of religion. The following four chapters summarize studies that were made for the specific purpose of examining in detail the relationships between various aspects of religious beliefs and activities and personal adjustment in old age.

Chapter 4

RELIGION AND PERSONAL ADJUSTMENT IN OLD AGE

THE MATERIAL PRESENTED in this chapter is based on a study of 219 persons aged sixty-five and over who were residents of seven institutions in the Minneapolis-St. Paul metropolitan area.[1] Five of these institutions are homes for the aged, and two are publicly supported homes which include younger infirm and indigent persons. For each of the 219 subjects of the study a lengthy questionnaire was filled out by an interviewer. More detailed case studies were made of a portion of the total group.

The questionnaire included the Burgess-Cavan-Havighurst Attitudes Inventory, which was used to measure personal adjustment in old age.[2] It consists of eight scales which may be used either to produce a composite personal adjustment score or to measure adjustment in each of the specific areas of health, friends, work, economic security, religion, feeling of usefulness, happiness and family. *Personal adjustment* is defined by this scale as satisfaction with activities and status, general happiness and a feeling of usefulness.[3]

Four major types of religious experience thought possibly to be related to personal adjustment in old age were analyzed. These were church membership, religious activities of the past and present, positions of leadership in the church or in church-related organizations and adherence to orthodox Christian beliefs in old age. In each case two groups of persons were compared. One had been exposed to the type of religious experience under consideration, and the other had not. Individuals

1. David O. Moberg, *Religion and Personal Adjustment in Old Age*, Ph.D. Thesis, University of Minnesota, Dec., 1951.

2. E. W. Burgess, R. S. Cavan and R. J. Havighurst, *Your Activities and Attitudes*, Science Research Associates, 1948.

3. R. S. Cavan, E. W. Burgess, R. J. Havighurst and H. Goldhamer, *Personal Adjustment in Old Age*, Science Research Associates, 1949, p. 111.

in the two groups were paired with one another on the basis of similarity of selected background characteristics so that the two groups were as much alike as possible except for the difference in the phase of religion that was the topic of the specific study.[4]

CHURCH MEMBERSHIP AND PERSONAL ADJUSTMENT IN OLD AGE[5]

Of the 219 subjects of this study, 132 were church members and eighty-seven were not at the time of interviewing. The church members had an average[6] personal adjustment score of 28.4 and the non-members 23.3 on the attitudes inventory. (The higher the score, the better the personal adjustment.) The better personal adjustment of the church members at the time of interviewing was statistically significant;[7] so great a difference could not normally have resulted from chance alone.

The church members of seven denominational groupings (Baptist, Catholic, Christian Science, Episcopal, Lutheran, Methodist and "all others") were compared with non-members who preferred the same denomination. In every case the members had higher personal adjustment scores. The superior adjustment of church members was also evident when the data were analyzed by sex, age, nativity, place of residence, years of schooling, marital and family status, self-rating of health, participation in social organizations and self-rating of happiness. When each of these was held constant, the church members had higher adjustment scores. The hypothesis that church membership is related to good personal adjustment in old age seemed by this evidence to be corroborated strongly.

4. This type of analysis is technically known as an *ex post facto experimental design.* It makes possible an approximation to a controlled experiment through indirect "mental" control by the experimenter rather than a direct manipulation of the individuals involved in the experiment. For discussions of the theoretical and logical bases and for illustrations of other applications of this research methodology, see F. Stuart Chapin, *Experimental Designs in Sociological Research,* Harper and Brothers, rev. ed., 1955, and Ernest Greenwood, *Experimental Sociology,* King's Crown Press, 1945.

5. David O. Moberg, "Church Membership and Personal Adjustment in Old Age," *Journal of Gerontology,* 8:207-211, Apr., 1953.

6. "Average" in this chapter refers to the arithmetic mean.

7. Statistical significance is generally at the one per cent level of confidence in this chapter, and never less than the five per cent level.

Fifty-three pairs of church members and non-members were then matched on the basis of sex, present employment or its absence, past and present club participation, marital status, number of living children, education and self-rating of health. The average personal adjustment score of the church members was 26.8 and that of the non-members 24.9. This was not a significant difference.

Because the differences in adjustment of the two groups had decreased as a result of careful matching, the members and non-members were compared on an even more rigorous basis. As a result of imposing two additional matching controls, nativity and place of residence at the time of interviewing, only nine pairs of persons remained. This increased the similarity of the backgrounds and reduced the personal adjustment scores of both groups, the church members' average score being 24.1 and the matched non-members' 24.2.

The lack of association between church membership and personal adjustment for these matched groups of individuals may reflect both the "quality" of church membership and the influence of the church on non-members. It is probable that many people join a church as a result of family influences and pressures without any personal convictions. This can be true of adult as well as childhood church joiners. Others may enter the church for various ulterior motives rather than because of a true religious commitment. If such church members could be distinguished from those who have come into the church as a result of genuine, personal, meaningful religious experiences and convictions, important differences might be found between the two groups, including differences in personal adjustment in old age.

We know that churches in America exert a definite influence on persons who are not members of them.[8] Many attend services regularly and take part in other church activities without ever becoming full members. In addition, the churches' influence often operates through persons who are church members to affect many secular activities both directly and indirectly, especially when moral and ethical standards are involved. Even non-members who have had nothing to do directly with the church may thus be influenced by it throughout their lives. Furthermore, because of the role of religion

8. John F. Cuber, "Marginal Church Participants," *Sociology and Social Research*, 25:57-62, Sept.-Oct., 1940.

in the historical development of our nation, the influence of the church is diffused throughout all areas of our social life. The indirect influence of the church may therefore be a partial source of the lack of significant differences in personal adjustment between the older church members and non-members who are the subjects of this study.

Some persons drop their church memberships in later life. Clifton's study of a random sample of old age assistance recipients in Minnesota indicated that many older people had dropped out of their churches, although churches held their members better than other organizations.[9] Such people have been under the church's direct influence in the past. Even if they are no longer members, they may have the same types of personal adjustment as those who are, if church membership is related to personal adjustment in old age.

Analysis of the subjects of our study tended to support this conclusion. The twenty-three non-members who did not indicate ever having been church members had an average personal adjustment score of 21.5, while the sixty-four non-members who had previously been church members had a score of 24.0. In the latter category, the thirty-two who had been members during part or most of their adult years had an average score of 25.5.

Individual pairing of the non-members who did not indicate ever having been church members with those who had once been members resulted in eleven matched pairs when seven control characteristics were used in the matching procedure (sex, education, marital status, number of living children, similar club activities in the past and present, self-rating of health and present lack of employment). The church members had an average score of 25.5, and the non-members 21.5, but this difference was not statistically significant.

The evidence from this study suggests the probability that the frequently observed relationship between church affiliation and good adjustment in old age is spurious or false. It is not church membership in and of itself that contributes to good personal adjustment in old age, at least in our nation where it is so easy to become a church member. The observed relationship must be due to other factors related to or accompanying religious affiliation.

9. C. Stanley Clifton, *A Study of the Leisure Time Interests and Activities of Old Age Assistance Recipients in Commercial Rest Homes in Minnesota*, Ph.D. Thesis, University of Minnesota, 1951.

RELIGIOUS ACTIVITIES AND PERSONAL ADJUSTMENT
IN OLD AGE[10]

A logical time to look for any relationship between religious
activities and adjustment of the individual is in old age. If
there is any such relationship, we can expect it to be most
evident after prolonged operation of the influence of religious
activities.

In the preceding chapter we noted several studies that found
certain religious activities to be related to good personal adjustment in old age. These findings, we observed, are only
fragmentary side-lights and subsidiary findings of the investigations of which they are a part.

To study this subject specifically, each of the 219 respondents was given a "religious activities score" on the basis of
present and past overt religious experiences. This score could
range from zero for a person who indicated no activity in
any of the eleven areas included to twenty-three for one who
indicated much activity in every one of them. The areas summarized by this score were church membership, present attendance at religious services, present attendance at religious services compared to attendance when about age fifty-five, attendance at religious services when about age twelve, positions and
offices held in the church, frequency of listening to religious
programs over the radio, reading from the Bible, reading other
religious books, private prayer, saying grace at meals during
most of the adult life and family prayers or some other form
of family worship during most of the adult life.

The religious activities score tended to discriminate against
non-church members in two ways: Church membership was itself one of the areas included, and the holding of offices is
usually limited by most churches to members. It also dis-
criminated against the infirm who were unable to attend, the
hard-of-hearing who could not hear religious radio services,
those with eyesight too poor to read the Bible, and the like.

Good personal adjustment and a high religious activities
score were found to be significantly correlated. A relationship
of this type, however, could result if persons who are well-
adjusted for other reasons than religious activities are the ones
who are religiously active, and vice versa. For instance, if all
persons who have a good education, good health, and living

10. David O. Moberg, "Religious Activities and Personal Adjustment in
Old Age," *Journal of Social Psychology*, 43:261-267, May 1956.

children are religiously active, and all those who have a poor education, poor health, and no living children are religiously inactive, then the relationship observed between personal adjustment and religious activities could be due entirely to these other factors and not to religion at all.

To hold constant some of the possible biasing characteristics related to personal adjustment in old age, persons with high religious activities scores (fifteen or higher) were matched with persons who had low scores (eight or less).

The eighty-six persons with high religious activities scores had an average personal adjustment score of 31.1, and the forty-one persons with low scores had an average score of 18.3. Members of the religiously "active" group (high religious activities scores) were paired with the "inactive" group (low scores) by the use of seven matching controls (sex, marital status, number of living children, education, present employment status, club activities, and self-rating of health). In addition, certain "secondary-control factors"[11] were used to increase the comparability of the two groups whenever there was a choice in the matching process of persons to retain.

The average personal adjustment scores of the paired individuals were 28.7 for the nineteen persons in the "active" group and 16.3 for those in the "inactive" group. This difference was not only statistically significant, but it was also found to prevail within each of the eight sub-areas that make up the personal adjustment attitudes inventory.

We may conclude, therefore, that either those who are well-adjusted engage in many religious activities, or that engaging in many religious activities contributes to good personal adjustment in old age.

CHURCH LEADERSHIP AND PERSONAL ADJUSTMENT IN OLD AGE[12]

In her study of one hundred persons over the age of sixty-five, Albrecht found that active social participation during the younger years seemed to contribute to good adjustment in old age. She also discovered that well-adjusted old people tended to withdraw into a more relaxed kind of participation instead

11. See David O. Moberg, "Two Problems of Experimental Designs," *The Midwest Sociologist*, Vol. 16, No. 1, pp. 10-12, Winter, 1954.
12. David O. Moberg, "Leadership in the Church and Personal Adjustment in Old Age," *Sociology and Social Research*, 37:312-316, May-June 1953.

of continuing to compete for status positions of high office or responsibility.[13]   Her findings suggest two things: Older persons who have held positions of leadership in the church in the past, a form of active social participation, may be better adjusted in old age than those who have not held such positions; and older people who cling to positions of leadership in the church may be less well-adjusted than those who no longer hold such positions.   (Purely honorary positions, such as the deaconship in certain churches, might be an exception to this.)

On the other hand, Burgess' has suggested the hypothesis that "downward vertical social mobility in old age is correlated with problems of adjustment in the later decades."[14]   This suggests the possibility that the older person who has once held a position of leadership in the church and then has been forced to relinquish it by ill health, declining physical vigor, social pressures, or other influences may be poorly adjusted in his old age.

Thirty-three of the 132 church members in our study were either Roman Catholic or Greek or Russian Orthodox. None of them still held a formal position of leadership in the church; four had held positions in the past, and two more had held only such minor positions as choir member and janitor. Of the ninety-nine Protestant church members, five still held one or more positions of leadership, thirty-five had held such positions only in the past, and four had held only minor positions.

The thirty-five Protestant church members who had held positions only in the past had an average personal adjustment score of 31.6, compared to a score of 27.2 for the fifty-five who did not indicate ever having held positions of church leadership. Eight control characteristics, in addition to Protestant church membership, were used to match comparable pairs in the two groups. These were sex, marital status, education, present employment status, number of living children, club activity, self-rating of health, and age within five years of each other. The twenty-two former church leaders had an average personal adjustment score of 31.5, and the matched non-leaders had a score of 27.0, a statistically significant difference. (The five who still held positions of leadership in the church had a score of 30.6.)

13. Ruth Albrecht, "The Social Roles of Old People," *Journal of Gerontology*, 6:144, Apr., 1951.
14. Ruth S. Cavan *et al., op. cit.*, p. 145.

It appears from these findings that taking an active part in church activities by assuming positions of leadership contributes to good personal adjustment in old age, even after these positions have been lost to the individual except in his memory. Perhaps this is because the older persons who were leaders in the past are still permitted or encouraged to give their advice and guidance to church activities through informal channels. If this is so, they may not feel they have lost social prestige and status within the group with the loss of office. Perhaps many of them retain their prestige within the group by virtue of their past services and accomplishments. Perhaps the tendency of many to desire to drop out of positions of leadership in old age and their accompanying voluntary withdrawal from them, together with the policy of many churches and church organizations to change leadership at regular intervals, also helps to prevent a lowering of personal adjustment when leadership positions are lost.

On the other hand, it is also possible that the personal adjustment of former leaders in the church was so good in the past that, even with a substantial lowering of it with the loss of leadership, they have adjustment scores that are superior to the rank and file of church membership.

The higher adjustment scores of former church leaders may reflect a causal relationship between personal adjustment in old age and the past holding of leadership positions in the church. It is also possible that some third factor or configuration of related factors may be the cause both of good personal adjustment and of being accepted as church leaders.

CHRISTIAN BELIEFS AND PERSONAL ADJUSTMENT IN OLD AGE[15]

Five items in the questionnaire dealt with prayer, sin, the future, the Bible, and Jesus. The answers to these were combined to form a single "religious belief score." The scoring, done by simple addition of weights representing various kinds of answers, made possible a highest score of ten and a lowest score of zero. A score of ten indicates a person who, at the time of interviewing, said he believed in heaven or a future life, believed in a prayer-answering God, believed that there

15. David O. Moberg, "Christian Beliefs and Personal Adjustment in Old Age," *Journal of the American Scientific Affiliation*, Vol. 10, No. 1, pp. 8-12, Mar., 1958.

is sin and that his own sins were forgiven, believed in the Bible as the perfect Word of God, and believed in Jesus Christ as the Savior who died a vicarious death. A score of zero designates a person who indicated no hope for the future, did not pray, did not believe in sin and its forgiveness, believed the Bible inspired only like other great pieces of literature, and believed Jesus to have been merely a great man.

For purposes of analysis, persons with high religious belief scores (seven through ten) were called "believers," and persons with low scores (zero through four) were called "non-believers." Some would classify "believers" as thus defined as conservative, fundamental, evangelical, or orthodox Christians, while the "non-believers" are more like non-Christians or like those sometimes called liberal or modernistic Christians, if they are members of Christian groups.

There is a serious limitation of this portion of the study: the tendency of many respondents to think to themselves, "What *ought* I to believe about this?" Sometimes this was outwardly expressed in the words, "What *should* I say?" or "What is the *right* answer?" When and if there were differences between the individual's personal beliefs and the conventional beliefs adhered to by his church, it is possible that the conventional answers tended to predominate; some persons seemed to be striving for consistency with their religious groups.

Religious beliefs were found to be closely associated with religious activities. There was a high correlation between the religious activities scores discussed previously in this chapter and the religious belief scores. This may be in part because prayer was an aspect of both scores, but it also reflects the probability that those who believe in the Bible as God's perfect Word are the most apt to read it reverently and consistently; and those who believe in Jesus as a vicarious Savior are the most likely to engage in the religious activities associated with Christian worship and praise.

Personal adjustment scores were also highly correlated with the religious belief scores, "believers" having higher adjustment scores than the "non-believers." However, "believers" in the highest belief score category who were not church members had higher personal adjustment scores than church members in the same category. Church members with low belief scores also tended to have lower personal adjustment scores than non-members with similar belief scores. This may indicate that deviant church members have guilty consciences because of the inconsistencies between their personal beliefs and their implicit profession of faith as church members.

The 155 "believers" had an average personal adjustment score of 28.0, and the thirty-five "non-believers" had a score of 19.9. The matching of individuals from the two groups by the use of seven controls (sex, self-rating of health, marital status, number of living children, education, present employment status, and similar past and present club activities) left twenty-two comparable persons in each group. The "believers" had an average personal adjustment score of 27.2 and the matched "non-believers" 19.9, a statistically significant difference.

Why should "believers" have better personal adjustment in old age? The "non-believer" who realizes death is approaching may be disturbed, at least sub-consciously, at the thought of dying and at his lack of assurance of a life beyond the grave. He may be bothered by feelings of guilt in not being certain his sins have been forgiven, even though he may *say* that he does not believe in sin. One person interviewed, for example, denied the existence of sin and then strongly affirmed her own sins had been forgiven.

The "believer" probably feels, conversely, a greater sense of usefulness than the "non-believer." Because he believes that God hears and answers his prayers, he thinks he can help others by interceding for them even when he is physically unable to offer any personal tangible or material assistance to those around him who are in need. Even though he recognizes his own sinfulness and lack of perfection, the "believer" may rejoice in his faith that the confession of his sins to God brings him forgiveness because of the vicarious sacrifice of Jesus Christ. He may be well-adjusted, even in the midst of suffering from physical infirmities and afflictions, because of his assurance that there is a purpose in everything that comes into his life. Even if only God knows that purpose, he has faith that God will make all things work together for his good. The adaptability and adjustability of the individual may be increased by his faith in such Biblical promises to the faithful as those expressed in Romans 8:28, Philippians 4:19, I Thessalonians 4:13-18, Hebrews 13:8, and I Peter 5:10.

On the other hand, the subjects of this study were reared in an era when the position of those we have called "believers" perhaps was more prevalent than it is among the present generation. It is possible that the religious beliefs imparted in one's childhood and youth give the greatest comfort and make for the best personal adjustment in old age. If so, children and youth reared in our current religious climate may experience the best personal adjustment in their future old age when they adhere to the type of religion they have been indoctrinated into during the early decades of life.

CONCLUSION

We have seen in this chapter that church membership in and of itself does not contribute to personal adjustment in old age, but that religious beliefs and activities possibly do. The engagement in many religious activities in childhood, adulthood and old age is correlated with good personal adjustment for the samples of older people that have been studied.[16] The holding of positions of leadership in the church during adulthood and adherence to the "faith of our fathers" in the later years are also associated with good adjustment in the closing years of life.

Needless to say, additional research is necessary to determine the extent to which these relationships are characteristic of all groups of older people and the degree to which they reflect cause-and-effect relationships between these various aspects of religion and personal adjustment in old age.[17] The conclusions reported in this chapter are based upon research on institutionalized old people. Indirect evidence both supports and contradicts the hypothesis that such findings may apply to all older people. Lepkowski, using the same basic measure of adjustment as that of this study, found no significant differences in personal or social adjustment between his samples of institutionalized and non-institutionalized Catholics over the age of sixty.[18] However, persons residing in old people's homes and those attending old age recreation centers in New York City have been observed to have differences in religious inter-

16. Another study of 37 institutionalized older persons resulted in similar findings. (Annette Burgess, Karin Jessup, and Carolyn Tenove, "The Relationship Between Religion and Personal Adjustment in Old Age," unpublished ms. in the files of D. O. Moberg, Bethel College, May 1960.)

17. Additional research suggestions are presented in the appendix.

18. J. Richard Lepkowski, "The Attitudes and Adjustments of Institutionalized and Non-institutionalized Catholic Aged," *Journal of Gerontology*, 11:185-191, Apr., 1956.

ests and activities.[19]   Concern with death was also found to be greater in a group of aging persons living in an institutional residence with more rigid authoritarian control than in a group of persons living in an apartment residence which approximates the normal opportunity for personal independence.[20] These findings suggest the possibility that the observed relationships between religion and personal adjustment in old age reported in this chapter may not apply equally to all groups of older people.[21]

19. Leo Chalfen, "Leisure-time Adjustment of the Aged: II. Activities and Interests and Some Factors Influencing Choice," *Journal of Genetic Psychology*, 88:261-276, June, 1956.

20. Samuel D. Shrut, "Attitudes toward Old Age and Death," *Mental Hygiene*, 42:259-266, 1958. Cf. Herman Feifel, "Older Persons Look at Death," *Geriatrics*, 11:127-130, Mar., 1956.

21. A recent study of a sample of 55 persons aged 65 and over who live independently in a middle-class urban community reveals that they achieved higher personal adjustment scores than the institutionalized persons who were the subjects of this chapter.   However, the same general pattern of relationships as reported in this chapter were observed between personal adjustment and church membership, religious activities, and religious beliefs. (Kathleen Renfrew, Jeanne Svendsen, Marie Valdas, and Joanne Williams, "Religion and Personal Adjustment in Old Age," unpublished paper, June 1, 1961.)

CHAPTER 5

PERSONAL ADJUSTMENT OF THE OLDER PERSON WITHIN THE CHURCH

IN THIS CHAPTER the result of an investigation of the personal adjustment of older persons in the church is reported.[1] The members studied were from two large churches in separate denominational groups in the Chicago area. Both are included in religious bodies with over 1,000,000 members in our nation.

This investigation was directed first toward determining if there is any difference in the personal adjustment of older (age sixty and over) and younger (ages fifty to fifty-nine) church members and second toward finding out if church members who are closely related to the church have better personal adjustment than members who are not so close to the church. Thirdly, the study sought to discover if church members increasingly turn to the church in old age when they meet the problem of making the transition to the later years. Finally, the investigation tried to locate those circumstances in the church experience that contributed to or hindered personal adjustment in old age. The results concerning the last objective are reported in the following two chapters; those concerning the first three problems are presented in this chapter.

PERSONAL ADJUSTMENT OF YOUNGER AND OLDER CHURCH MEMBERS

Other studies have indicated that there is a shift toward religion in the later decades of life.[2] These investigations

1. Robert M. Gray, *A Study of the Personal Adjustment of the Older Person in the Church*, unpublished Ph.D. dissertation, University of Chicago, 1953. See also Robert M. Gray, "The Personal Adjustment of the Older Person in the Church," *Sociology and Social Research*, 41:175-180, Jan.-Feb., 1957.
2. See Chapter 3 for a summary of these studies.

point out that older persons generally have favorable attitudes toward religion which become more intense with the aging process. They further indicate that some church-related activities increase with advancing age. It is, therefore, plausible to suppose that the individual turns to the church partly to alleviate anxieties and tensions regarding death and to receive comfort and reassurance, since the church offers some compensatory adjustment for tensions in other spheres.

If the church member turns to the church in later life to find satisfaction and alleviation of anxieties from tensions, we might expect this to have some effect on his personal characteristics and activities. It would be useful, therefore, to determine the nature of this influence, whether favorable or unfavorable. It seems valid to assume that church membership alone would not offset the continuous trend toward less favorable personal adjustment among older persons but would tend to retard the process and that the church member would be more active and have more favorable characteristics in the various age-groups than the non-member.

A consideration central to this proposition is the assumption that the person who has enjoyed an active role in the church program will be in a much more favorable position to adjust in old age than the person who is not a church member. The personality of the older person is not a product simply of old age but grows out of his earlier personality.[3] A person who has been closely affiliated with the church for a life time, or a long period of time, will have established a role and status in the church which continues even though activities in other spheres are curtailed. If he is close to the church, one would expect that he has enjoyed the fruits of the program designed, among other things, to aid him develop a healthy and wholesome personality. Still further, one may assume that the individual will have developed ties and bonds within the church and will have many friendships and relationships which will not necessarily end at retirement but will continue to flourish and satisfy. It may also be postulated that church experience provides compensations and satisfactions for the tensions and anxieties resulting in other areas and performs a valuable function in alleviating problems of old age and aiding in the adjustment of the older person in society.

3. R. S. Cavan, E. W. Burgess, R. J. Havighurst and H. Goldhamer, *Personal Adjustment in Old Age*, Science Research Associates, 1949, p. 35.

The foregoing observations set forth a number of factors common to contemporary church groups which would seem to lend plausibility to the supposition that membership in a church group does aid the individual in making the transition from middle age to old age. Similarly, it would appear reasonable to assume that older persons who are church members will not develop as serious personality adjustment problems as is apparently the case with older people in general, but that they will in fact have as favorable personality adjustment as younger members who are approaching but have not yet reached old age.[4]

The general hypothesis was tested through examination of data concerning the church members which utilized thirty-one items from the Activity and Attitude Schedule which together make up a criterion for measuring personal adjustment.[5] One should expect, under the hypothesis, to find no significant differences concerning these factors between the older and younger persons in the study group.

The analyses of data relevant to the thirty-one factors used as a reliable measure of personality adjustment revealed that there were no major differences in personal adjustment between the older and younger members studied in either church congregation. The persons aged sixty and over as well as the younger members between fifty and fifty-nine were enjoying good personal adjustment. This is not necessarily the case with other oldsters in this country, as we know from various scientific studies.

CLOSENESS TO THE CHURCH AND PERSONAL ADJUSTMENT

The opportunities furnished by organized religion for satisfying the needs of older persons are manifold and extend into

4. *Ibid.*, p. 8. Cavan has stated: "Although it is possible, as we have seen, to state theoretically the criteria of functional old age, exact means of measuring these criteria have not yet been developed." For purposes of analysis we have used sixty years, as did Cavan, as the age period designating "later maturity" in the old age group. This procedure permits the inclusion of certain persons who age earlier than others as well as those who are experiencing old age at present. At the same time, we have placed persons between fifty and fifty-nine years of age in the "younger" age group category.

5. Ethel Shanas, *The Personal Adjustment of Recipients of Old Age Assistance: With Special Consideration of the Methodology of Questionnaire Studies of Older People,* Unpublished Ph.D. Dissertation, Department of Sociology, University of Chicago, 1949.

many areas of life. In spite of the fact that the church has shared to some extent the prevailing attitudes of our times toward older people, it can safely be said that the church is vitally interested in the older person and has a place for him. From a Christian standpoint the Gospel makes no age distinctions between children of God. This is not necessarily the situation in other social institutions where changes in capacity which accompany old age are of prime importance in determining attitudes toward and positions of older persons.

Another reason why church membership may possibly be of importance to adjustment in later maturity is that the person who has enjoyed an active role in the church program has experienced life-long personality development in it. He will be in a much more favorable position to adjust in old age than the non-member, if this is true.

A further important function of church experience which may benefit personal adjustment in old age is that the individual in the church develops friendships and ties that do not end at retirement but continue to flourish and satisfy. This is an obvious contribution toward the adjustment and happiness of the older church member.

In addition to these factors, there are other phenomena with regard to the church that may be presumed to aid adjustment in old age. It is generally agreed by physicians, psychiatrists and social scientists that many thwarted personalities, unhappy persons and illnesses are a result of negative emotions, such as anxiety, worry, apprehension and fear. These emotions cause spasms of a muscular, nervous or glandular nature which, when and if continued for any extended length of time, sometimes result in psychosomatic illnesses, frustrations, irritations and maladjustments. It is further agreed that one of the best ways to overcome these conditions is to replace negative emotions with more positive ones, namely, joy, contentment, satisfaction, security, etc. One way that the church may contribute to this process, and at the same time aid in personal adjustment, is to provide compensations and satisfactions to release the tensions and anxieties resulting in other areas of life. Finally, the church provides a wholesome environment conducive to the development of the positive emotional tone so necessary to happiness and adjustment in any period of a person's life.

The foregoing observations in conjunction with other findings reported in this book set forth a number of factors common to contemporary church groups which would seem to indicate the importance of church membership to personal adjustment in old age.   It is possible, however, to project this study further and to develop information which gives even more valuable data in our quest to develop information concerning whether or not church membership is important to adjustment in old age.   The personal adjustment of persons who are closely affiliated with the church can be compared with that of members who are not so close to the church.

Our analysis has indicated the importance of church membership to older persons, but we have not developed specific information concerning the relationship between the degree or intensity of church membership and personal adjustment.   If it is true, as studies reported in Chapters 3 and 4 suggest, that church membership and associated religious characteristics tend to aid a person's adjustment during the later years, then this positive influence should be commensurate with the degree of integration into the church fellowship or closeness of church membership.   Obviously it would not be expected that a person who maintains loose ties with the church would receive the same benefits as the member who is close to the church.

Analysis of the data revealed that persons who were close to the church had, as a group, slightly better personal adjustment than comparable members not so closely affiliated.   This is added evidence that the church does contribute to good personal adjustment in old age.   Another significant finding was that only five out of a total of 296 older church members reported themselves as being poorly adjusted.

In conclusion, we may safely state that our analysis has revealed that the church plays a positive role in personal adjustment in old age.   An overwhelmingly large majority of our church membership had "average or better" adjustment, and closely affiliated members had slightly better personal adjustment than the non-close members.   In order to test this assumption, closely affiliated and non-close church members of the two church groups were compared with respect to personal adjustment.[6]

6. Closeness to the church was determined by using the Church Activities Section of the schedule, *A System of Measuring Common Social Roles of Elderly People* by Ruth Albrecht, University of Chicago.

ACTIVITY IN AND ATTITUDE TOWARD THE CHURCH IN LATER YEARS

An analysis also sought to determine if church members increasingly turn to the church in old age when meeting the problem of making the transition to the later years.

The analysis of the data relative to the two church groups revealed approximately the same findings for both males and females. There were no differences between the younger and older men in either church group with respect to church activities and attitude toward religion. The women in both study groups, except for two items, did not significantly differ. Older women tend to read their Bibles and listen to church radio services more frequently than younger female members.

The conclusion is that older persons who are already church members fit right in and have their basic needs met without increasing their activities and dependence upon the church. The findings suggest that it is better for a person to become active in the church in his early years than to turn to the church and religion only upon meeting the problems of old age.

CHAPTER 6

CONTRIBUTIONS OF THE CHURCH TO ADJUSTMENT

THE RELATION OF THE CHURCH to successful aging involves a number of factors, both negative and positive. In this chapter and the next attention is turned to a description of some of these factors, together with circumstances which have been involved in the personal adjustment of church members in later life.

The analysis is based upon concrete case materials obtained in personal interviews with forty-eight persons.[1] They were carefully selected from the church groups discussed in the previous chapter to represent categories of age, sex, and closeness of church affiliation. The interviews were conducted with as little direction as possible by the interviewer; the average duration of each was about two and one-half hours. Notes were taken during the interview, and a more thorough transcript was made immediately following it.

These interviews are not presented in statistical form because the foregoing chapters have adequately established the association between the church experience and personal adjustment in old age. These data are to be thought of as supplementary to the statistical materials of the previous chapter and concern specific areas suggested by the conceptual scheme of the Social Science Research Council's Committee on Old Age.[2] Our task here is to present further insights concerning data that have already been objectively reported. We do not intend to evolve an exhaustive classification of the areas in which the church

1. Robert M. Gray, *A Study of the Personal Adjustment of the Older Person in the Church*, unpublished Ph.D. dissertation, University of Chicago, 1953. See also Robert M. Gray, "The Personal Adjustment of the Older Person in the Church," *Sociology and Social Research*, 41:175-180, Jan.-Feb., 1957.

2. Otto Pollak, *Social Adjustment in Old Age, A Research Report*, Social Science Research Council, 1948, p. 162.

contributes to adjustment or maladjustment; we do intend to signify, by selection and emphasis, those which have been of obvious importance to the adjustment of the persons whose experiences are reported.

These data are to be viewed as suggestive only. They represent personal illustrations of and possible explanations for the findings previously reported. We make no pretentions that these few statements adequately represent the negative and positive values of the church experience, nor do we assert that these data can be generalized to other groups. This will necessarily depend upon further empirical research upon each of the factors. The adjustment value items are presented in this chapter and the maladjustment data in the following one.

"The opportunities furnished by organized religion for satisfying needs of older people are manifold and extend from the sphere of religion proper to other areas."[3]

The following sections include cases and quotations representative of the study's findings concerning adjustment values of experiences in the church. They indicate that the church indeed did satisfy needs beyond the sphere of religion proper. It alleviated anxieties concerning death, provided companionship and an environment for continuing friendships, gave opportunities for participation in a social group in which the older person was welcome, assisted adjustment to the death of loved ones, furnished comfort in times of discouragement and crisis, met spiritual needs by coming to the person no longer able to come to church and satisfied basic social and psychological needs.

THE CHURCH ALLEVIATES ANXIETY CONCERNING DEATH

The church by providing comfort and reassurance alleviates the individual's anxiety concerning approaching death. The anxiety concerning the approach of death appears to be related to several motives. First of all, the desire to live and to continue living is apparent in most individuals, regardless of age.[4] Although many persons have a general fear of the death

3. *Ibid.*
4. Otto Pollak, *op. cit.*, p. 161. It is also true, however, that persons beyond 75 years of age are less worried about dying than about becoming a burden to relatives or society through illness, disability or poverty. (John E. Anderson, "Placing the Adult Years in Proper Perspective in Development Through the Life Span," in *The Middle Years*, Proceedings of the Sixth Annual Iowa Conference on Gerontology, Iowa City, 1957, p. 6.)

process or of death itself, belief in the hereafter tends to mitigate these fears. It is also true that religious teachings concerning punishments and rewards after death may create a considerable amount of anxiety concerning the afterlife. Finally, there may be concern over the fate of dependents who would be left without support. These factors and how the church experience affects them are illustrated in the following excerpts from interview records.

A man, aged seventy-five, living with his invalid wife who had recently suffered a stroke, spoke as follows:

Neither my wife nor myself has any fear of death. When it comes it comes; that is all there is to it and, of course, we believe in an after-life which helps us meet this common problem. When my wife first had her stroke we thought that she was going to die — we were both ready and unafraid.

A retired man who was living in his own home described his attitude toward approaching death as follows:

I'm seventy-six years of age and realize that I can't live forever. Why I might be gone tomorrow. I hope that when I do go the Lord will be good to me and let death come quickly. I have faith that this will be the case with me. After death I don't know exactly what will happen but I know my soul will go to heaven if I don't do anything wrong between now and then. I've lived a good life and set a good example for my children.

A woman living in a private home stated that no one will ever know what the church has meant to me." She expressed her attitude toward death in the following manner:

While I'm not positive about the resurrection of the body I am certain there is an after-life. As far as hell and damnation are concerned, my conception of God is that he would never condemn us — we condemn ourselves and I'm sure that I have not done this as I have tried to live a good Christian life. I like life very well but will not and do not fear death.

A man, eighty years of age, who had been retired for quite a few years, was supporting his wife and himself by running a mail-order business. He said he had planned on this job years earlier because "I knew if I didn't work I'd dry up and die." His feelings toward death, which he didn't expect for a long time, were expressed as follows:

I'm not worried about death because I don't expect to die for years to come. I'm in good physical condition. How old do you think I am, young man? Well, I'm eighty and have taken good care of myself all of my life and it's been the church teachings which have aided me to do these things.

I've got a brother in the hospital who has lived the kind of

life that I admire, honest, married, church member and kind —
but he is dying at only sixty-eight. He got to eating a lot and
got stout and this worked on his heart and it has gone back on
him and he is in an oxygen tent now.

I believe in God and everlasting life but how it will be no
one knows. But I do know that I will see my brother again.

A married man in comfortable circumstances had long been
a member of the church and was prepared for and not afraid
of death and the hereafter. He said:

I never fear death, and this is directly on account of my religious beliefs. I'm not a fatalist and I know that life has a meaning and that there is a purpose to it all. I've had a wonderful
life and my wife and I share everything together. I believe I'll
go to dust like the Bible reads, and in the hereafter I can answer
the questions just like I have done for you. When my father
died at seventy-six years of age, he was an active Christian, probably better than I am, the minister came to give him the last
communion and father just told him that he didn't believe this
was necessary because one would be judged according to his life
while on the earth. This is also my belief and I have lived a
good Christian life and have no fear of death or the hereafter.

A concern for those left behind, even though sure of meeting again in the hereafter, was expressed by a male member
as follows:

Am I worried about death? Certainly not. I don't want to
die if that is what you mean, but I am not worried about it other
than leaving the wife not well cared for. You see we haven't
always had it so good and for about three years there we had a
lot of sickness and now we are paying for it, and I wouldn't
want to die now and leave all these bills for my wife. Yes, I
believe I will meet my wife in the hereafter. If I didn't believe
in the hereafter, I wouldn't be going to church. This is my only
worry about death; other than that there is nothing to fear, only
I hope to live a long time yet.

An elderly man who was quite ill at the time of the interview and had been so for a long time, stated that he was particular about trying to get to church on Sunday because "this
is the most important thing in my life." He also said that
he got much consolation from the church regarding his sickness and the hereafter:

The church means everything to me and I am very particular
about getting there each Sunday if I can make it. I am ancient
and it seems impossible that I am this old. Going to church is
the most important thing in my life. With regards to how I
feel about death and the hereafter, I would like to live longer
but I have no fear of death. I just take it for granted what

I've been taught all of my life and what I understand is true and do not fear when my turn comes. It's hard to say definitely just what will happen — I don't really know, as no one definitely knows, about the hereafter. All we can do is live a good clean life and depend on the Lord and he will take care of you. It's a consolation to me to know this.

The following remarks were made by a woman whose husband had been crippled by arthritis, bringing much unhappiness to them. Like other members in somewhat different circumstances, she indicated how important church membership had been in alleviating fear of impending death:

I have always been active in the church and would have been lost without my church membership. It has many times been all that my husband and I have had to fall back on and that's the way it is now. I have no worry about death. I feel this way as I have been taught all my life that this life is a prelude before death which leads to a new and wonderful life. I hope that I am an over-comer. If not I will not make as much a grade as I want. But I love the Lord and am grateful to him for the sacrifice he made for me and for others whereby all can be saved if they accept him as their Savior.

The explanation of this woman is typical of nearly all persons interviewed in that they expressed a concern for rewards and punishments in the after-life. Apparently she like the others finds solace and comfort in her faith in the Savior and in having lived a good Christian life, which traditionally has been regarded by many church men as the way to salvation.

A woman who has been a member of the church nearly all her life and whose husband was still living said:

The church means everything to me and if I couldn't go I wouldn't feel right all week. I love the people there and the beautiful spirit which is so comforting to both my husband and myself. The church helps me to know there is a God and that there is a life after. I'm not very good at explaining things but I feel it in my heart. Everyone who believes in an after-life believes in God. I believe in a beautiful after-life and that is what I like about the church. We know there is a God from so many proofs.

A male member spoke of his belief in the life to come and his desire to continue after death:

I think about death often. I have been very close to death on four different occasions. I'm not afraid to die although I have a lot to live for. Death doesn't hold any fear for me because I'll meet many old friends. Death is just a natural part of my eternal life.

A woman whose husband at one time had been a church leader referred to her anxiety concerning the pain and suffering which sometimes accompany death.

> I don't worry about death because it will come to all of us sometime and there is a beautiful life after this one. Only thing I don't want to be sick for a long time or suffer or be a nuisance to anyone. These are the only things that bother me because I'm sure of the others.

This woman had no fears regarding the hereafter but was concerned lest she experience pain and suffering prior to death. This was mentioned by many others and indicates one area in which the church does not mitigate anxieties related to death to any great extent.

An elderly man, aged eighty, expressed the thought that death will be a beautiful thing for him because he will once again be united with his loved ones who have all previously passed away.

> I have no fear of death; it can come any day to me. It's only a change over death to life. I know I am worthy to be resurrected. Christ was the first of all the children of God to be brought up and someday I will do likewise. I thank you, God! I am the last of the family and am looking forward to meeting all my loved ones again. I know we will all be together again.

An aged woman stated that death to her meant passing on into a new world where she would be with all of her friends again, but she expressed a concern for those she would leave behind.

> Death will soon come now. I'm not worrying about it. I know I have many friends in the other world waiting until I get there. My kids are raised so I don't have to worry about them, and I hope and pray that they will be all right.

A similar instance of not fearing death because it would be a time of reunion with loved ones and friends was depicted by a woman who had never married and lived alone with her aged father in a small apartment behind the store she managed.

> I don't worry about death. When I die I am going to look for mother and my dear sisters. I am going to see how they feel and act. They were just as good as I, and we are anxious to meet them.

This woman was not able to go to church because of the necessity of keeping her store open on Sundays. She indicated the value of the church in alleviating anxieties regarding death and the hereafter in persons unable to participate in church activities.

I never get to go to church because I have to keep open on Sundays or I would soon be out of business. Although I can't go to church the church leaders come here to visit me very often and they nearly always give me a lesson. Besides, I learned all about the church before and I still have my church books and prayer. I'm still close to the church and know I will live again after this life.

Another woman with a similar conviction expressed her belief in a hereafter and indicated she had lived a good Christian life and was prepared to go whenever the call came.

I think about death often. I don't worry about it. We all are born to die because we can't live forever. I have faith that I will because I have lived a good Christian life and have been a good lady. I haven't a selfish bone in my body and what I have had, I shared with others. Yes, I'm prepared to die and am not afraid.

These cases could be supplemented by others which demonstrate the value of the church in alleviating anxiety concerning death through provision of comfort and reassurance. The illustrative material revealed that the church members' fear of death was diminished through belief in an after-life which they had acquired through the church. They felt, for the most part, that they had lived good Christian lives and would have nothing to fear in the life to come.

THE CHURCH PROVIDES COMPANIONSHIP AND A SETTING FOR CONTINUED FRIENDSHIPS

One of many factors which contribute to good personal adjustment is having a number of enduring intimate and personal friends. The church offers the individual an opportunity to participate in an atmosphere conducive to finding companionship which will not end at an arbitrary age as is so in many other spheres of life. The church member has many friendships which endure over a period of many years and has the opportunity to continue making new friends.

The materials presented here pertain to these friendships and the value of the church in providing companionship and a setting for continuous friendships.

The first case is that of a married man eighty years of age who had been retired from his job five years.

I have belonged to my church since 1900 when I was a young man and moved here from the west side of Chicago. What I like about the church best is the associations. I meet more honest and better people in the church than outside. All of my friends are in the church.

This subject's remarks exemplify an attitude manifested by nearly all of the subjects interviewed. This was an appreciation of the many friendships to be found within the church.

A widow remarked:

> The church is wonderful. The thing that helps me is the many friendships which I have developed since I became a member some thirty years ago. I belong to many of the church organizations and have many friends. I haven't been too well because I worked too hard helping my husband before he died, and because of this I don't take a too active part anymore. I still go over and visit my friends as often as possible. This is one thing that is worthwhile for older persons and that is to belong to a church and other organizations where you can meet and enjoy friends.

Maintaining friendships was one of the primary functions of the church for this woman; it was the first thing she mentioned when asked the value of church membership to her.

Another woman who expressed an appreciation for the many fine friends that she had in the church stated that one of the most important functions of the church was to provide a place where a person can go and find good wholesome companionship regardless of how old or young one is. She said:

> Church is important and I don't see how anyone can get by without the church and the associations which it provides. It gives us an uplift for the rest of the week which we miss so much if we do not attend. I am happy my daughter is interested in the church. We have a wonderful group of people at our church and it makes you so happy to go out and meet them during the week. I believe that this association is the most important function of the church in that it provides activities and friendships for everyone and there are so many lonely oldsters. I wish we could bring them all to church; I know they would be much happier.

Finding help through friendships in the church was the theme of a well educated woman member.

> I needed help at one time in my life and I did not know what to do. I was given a spiritual vision that God was my Father and that He is ever with me. This gave me much comfort when my husband was so sick in the hospital. When I went over to the church everyone was so nice to me they just welcomed me into all of their activities. I thought at first they were just being kind because my husband was sick but later found that they were so to everyone. I appreciate more than I can say the friendship that I found in the church.

This experience of going to the church in time of trouble and finding there a rich source of friendship also was expressed by a woman who had been very active in her younger years but had stayed away recently because of the illness of her husband.

I would have been lost without my church membership. I have always been active in the church. In fact I was once a missionary. We haven't been to church lately; my husband is too ill. The women are wonderful and I love every one of them. I went there a stranger but they accepted me right away and they invited me into a circle. They all love my husband and I thought it was because of him but it was because they love me. This made me so happy that I went home and cried for a long time. I am never lonely because I go to all the association meetings and meet all the wonderful women.

An old man, eighty years of age, who went to church twice on Sunday and tried to participate in as many church activities as possible, replied to a question concerning the value of the church to him in the following manner:

The only happiness in the world is in the church. When you are close to God you have to chase bad ideas away all the time. You can't help it if a bird flies over your head but if it nests there it is your fault. I do have most of my friends over there and have known most of them for many years and would not know what to do if I couldn't see them once in a while. I don't like to tell my troubles to other people but when I do have them it makes me feel better to get out and mingle with other people. I guess the church is the only place I know of where I can go and talk to others without feeling out of place. I do have a friend down the street who I try to visit once every day and we have good times talking together but other than that all of my friends are in the church.

A school teacher offered an explanation of the value of the church which is typical of many others:

The best thing in life is to have friends. I don't care who you are or what you do; unless you have many friends and have the opportunity to get out and mix with other people you will never be entirely happy. That is the main reason why so many of your older persons are so unhappy today . . . they don't have any place to go and they do not have anything to do with their spare time. Idleness is the devil's workshop and most of the people spend too much time without doing anything. I think the church is the answer to this problem. I go there and enjoy the friendship of numerous persons who I know live good and appreciate me. We all feel the same way at church. It's too bad that the rest of the people don't have the same experience. I have taught school for years right here in this city and I know that this would be good for the young people as well as the older ones. You've got to have good friends to be happy and you also have to have something to do with your spare time.

A married woman mentioned the value of the many friends that she had in the church, saying that she had built her whole life around it. This woman who had become a member forty-one years earlier stated that in any church one would meet better friends than if he were not a member.

> The church has been an incentive for me to get ahead. Those who don't belong to a church never seem to get ahead. I think you will have better companions and associates in the church, and from the way conditions are today this is the only place where you ought to meet your friends. Of course there are many fine people who are not church members but by and large people who go to church are generally good people. The friends that I have at church are an essential part of my life and I would not like to be without them.

This statement expresses a common attitude among church members; they desire to cultivate wholesome friendships in a healthy environment and believe that the church is a good place to do this.

One woman mentioned that she thought that the friendships were as important as the spirit in the church.

> The church means everything to me and I think that if I couldn't go to church I wouldn't feel right at all. The two most important things that I find when I go there are my many friends and the spirit which is always present. These are what I would miss most if I for some reason or other could not go to church.

An elderly man who had spent twenty-five or more years working with young boys in the church added that he thought that working with the Boy Scouts and cultivating the many friendships had done more than anything else to make his life happy.

> The church has brought peace of mind to me and I have learned that there is a God and this has helped me over many of the problems that I have had to meet in life. The thing in the church that has meant most to me is working with the boys and meeting the many wonderful people that it has been my privilege to associate with all of these years. I don't know how my life would have been without this but I do know that I have been ever so happy, and I am certain that my relationships with the boys and the many fine people that I have met while I have been a member of the church have meant more to me than anything that I can think of.

An elderly lady stated that the only people who were ever nice to her any more were her friends in the church.

I don't have any relatives because they have all died and I am alone except for my friends in the church. I would like to sing in the choir over there but no one ever asks me, but I guess they want that for the young people. I love the church and the people there. Most of them are real nice to me. They are the only people that I know who try to be nice to me. Even my landlord does not try to be nice to me and I try to be nice to her. Over at church I meet lots of people. If you don't feel welcome there, it's your own fault. If you smile others will smile back at you. If you come with a long face, they will act that way back to you and pass you by. I shake hands with everyone, and I won't let them pass me by. It makes us all happy and they won't pass me by. If you belong to a lodge, people are friendly there I suppose, but when you get old, people are not nice to you except in church where we are brothers and sisters. I praise soldiers and sailors about how they are giving their life for mine. They love me for it. I love to go to church every week.

Another aged woman offered a somewhat different reason why she appreciated her friendships in the church:

I do love companionship and I do miss the church. I fell down the cellar stairs and injured myself and now I can't make the trip. I am now fearful of stairs and can't stand streetcars because they nauseate me and I get very nervous. Besides I could not afford the expense of going to church. I guess I am quite a problem. I love music and singing so much and my voice is still clear and I wish that I could go and still sing in the choir. Even though I can't go any more many of my friends come here to visit me. They have never forgotten me. This is about all I have to live for outside of caring for my blind sister. They come here and fix up the house for me and watch out for us all the time. My friends from the church are the only ones who ever come to see me except my son and his wife.

These illustrative materials were assembled to depict the role of the church in providing a setting for friendships and a place where a person can find companionship in a wholesome environment. These few cases do not encompass all of the instances wherein church members expressed the value of the church experience in providing friendships, but they are sufficient to illustrate this function of the church.

THE CHURCH PROVIDES OPPORTUNITY TO PARTICIPATE IN A SOCIAL ENVIRONMENT IN WHICH THE OLDER PERSON IS WELCOME

Another important function of the church which assuredly contributes to good adjustment is that it provides many types of activities. These give members an opportunity to take part in one or more programs, depending upon personal interests and desires. Furthermore, these activities do not end upon reaching a certain age but continue as long as the person is able and desires to participate. The church makes no unkind distinction between age groups. In it the older person finds an opportunity to work and to be part of a social environment in which he is welcome, as is not necessarily the case in other social institutions. The following excerpts from interview records illustrate the salutary influences of this service of the church.

A married man living with his wife indicated that his church activities took up all of his spare time, for which he was very grateful.

> The church has always meant a great deal to me and my family. I was brought up with a strict religious background and I have never fell off from that. I have never placed denomination first; as we raised our family, the children and my wife and I would attend the church closest to our home. I have spent my whole life working in the church and even now when I am not able to get around too good I am still active. I've been active as a trustee and ruling Elder for some eight years. I don't take a real active part any more like teaching in the Sunday school. I am Chairman of Benevolences and past president of the Men's Club and am active in the organization of the Men's Council. Throughout my life the church has taken nearly all of my spare time and I know that this has made my life better because so many persons spend their time being idle or doing bad things. I am happy I joined the church because it has given me something to do even now when I am old and can't do much of anything else.

A single man, living with his sister in a private home, described his appreciation for the small jobs that he was permitted to take care of at the church.

> I am not married and because of this and other reasons I am not especially strong in the social end of the church. I've always been connected with the running of it though. I am on the Board of Trustees and on the Housing Committee at the present time. Whenever they need repairs it is my job to go and size up the job. I suppose that they could get someone else who could do the job better but I have been doing this job for a long long time and most of them believe that I am still the best man for the job. I feel that if I just pulled out from church activities it would ruin me.

His sister stated that he was a very sick man and was supposed to keep quiet and not engage in any strenuous activities at all, yet he wouldn't stay home from his church job because, according to him, that was what he lived for now that he was too old to do anything else. She had tried to get him at least to slow down on his church job, but he gave the following reason why he didn't wish to do so:

> It is too much pleasure for me to look after things over at the church. It's a little heavy work for me at my age but it's fun even though I worry about it all the time. I enjoy it very much; otherwise I wouldn't do it, and they seem to be glad I do it. Several fellows over there are very enthusiastic about it and no one has mentioned getting a younger man to take over, at least they have not said anything to me.

One man said that he had had his share of hard luck and had found refuge in the church. He now went to church because he enjoyed the many activities and associations that he found there.

> I feel very welcome over at the church and more so than any place that I know of. I get much happiness in going and meeting with all my friends and associates there. Sunday without church would be meaningless. There is a material as well as a spiritual satisfaction in going to the church. We get to take part in many activities and I know of many older persons who don't have any other social life but what they get at the church. I know that I will always enjoy my friends and the activities at the church and I don't care much what happens on the outside because the church takes very good care of its members. In fact all of our social needs are satisfied by the church and its activity.

A well-to-do woman, devoted to her husband and children, was so busy in caring for her home and making things comfortable for her family that she had few outside activities except those which she enjoyed in the church.

> I don't get to participate in many social activities in the community, and the reason I don't go too often is that my family takes up all of my time. When I am through caring for them I don't have time for anything else. I do participate in some church activities and I belong to an association and a church circle which I try to attend regularly. This is the extent of my social life.

A woman who had experienced serious family troubles had found refuge in the church, especially in its activities.

> My mom was a neurotic and she didn't get along with me at all. While I took care of the family I had a very sad life and the church was my salvation because it gave me strength to go on. At one time I even wanted to go on a mission to China to keep active and to keep my mind off of things, but I never got to go because I did not have the money. Mother used to get sore at

me when I would go to church, but I would get up and prepare the meals and just go — it was my only salvation. No one knows what it meant to me then and what it means to me now to be able to participate in the church where I know that I am respected and wanted. I have been active in the church ever since I joined. I have taught many Sunday-school classes and enjoyed the social life. I was a church staff visitor for ten years and worked with the young people for a long time. I have been also very active in the women's work and president of a number of organizations. I put in all my time there at the church to the exclusion of activities and friendships anywhere else.

A retired man of seventy-six, living only with his wife, expressed his appreciation in being able to go to church for recreation and something to do with his spare time.

I am hard of hearing and for this reason I have not been a leader over at the church, but I have worked on many church activities. I always go out on Christmas and Thanksgiving to visit the poor people and go over to the old folks club parties all the time. That sure is a good idea giving us something to do. I really appreciate their efforts and am so much more happy there than I would be in a tavern.

A woman who evidently was greatly concerned about her daughter expressed deep satisfaction that the church offered such a wide range of activities for young and old alike.

All of our needs are satisfied in the church, such as friendships, social and mental security. Our daughter was raised in a rough high school and yet all of her friends are church members, and this has given my husband and me so much comfort. We all try to participate in all the church activities and in this way hope to keep our family together and happy.

Another woman said that the church and its activities were her whole life.

The church has meant everything to me, and I don't know what I would have done without it. I have been active all of my life and was practically raised in the church. I am an officer in our circle and my husband is a trustee. We get so much joy and comfort from the church that I suppose that this is our whole life.

A woman, sixty-two years of age, stated simply her love for the church and the fact that she felt welcome in it.

I do love the church and all the people there. I enjoy the minister and his messages which he gives us each Sunday. It is so enjoyable to take part in the church activities and to know that you are loved and appreciated as well as being wanted. I know that this isn't so in other organizations that I have belonged to during my life.

A man who had been a church member all of his seventy-five years of life mentioned how he felt welcome at church and liked to take part in its activities.

I go to church every Sunday and every chance I get on other days. They make me feel welcome at church and I make them feel welcome. I like to meet the strangers and to make them feel right at home because I know how much it means to someone to be made felt welcome. . . . In my day I have done a lot of work at the church. I have never been lonesome at the church because I make it my business to talk to people. I'm a good one to mingle with people but I don't force myself, but I do love to meet people. About the only place I know of to do this is over at the church.

An elderly woman disclosed that all of her time was devoted to the church and that she didn't know what she would do if she didn't have her church.

I have been a member of the church all my life. My husband and I have worked all of our lives in the church. I hate to think what we would do without the church as there would be a void in our lives without it. There is development of every kind in it and especially when you grow older because the members respect the older persons in the church a lot more than they do on the outside. I had an operation and had to stop many of my church activities but there are still plenty of things to do to keep me busy all the time.

A man who regularly attended church expressed a common feeling among many older members:

I feel very welcome at the church. There are so many new faces and most are young members. I've always been one to want to meet people at church. I love to participate in the church because I know that I am loved by my brothers and sisters as I love them because we are one big happy family. It's truly wonderful.

A lady spoke as follows:

I hope I always feel as welcome at church as I do today and know that I will. I never feel lonely over there with all those wonderful people.

A woman who had lived in relative poverty mentioned that she and her husband found satisfaction participating in the church activities where it didn't make any difference how rich a person was:

I don't have anything, and that is why I have to lean so much on the Lord. My church is my staff. We haven't had it so good and my husband has worked hard but never made much and I have had to work much of my life. When we go to church we feel quite comfortable even though neither my husband nor myself are the active type. They work hard to make it nice for us.

We enjoy all of the activities and know we are just as welcome as are those members who have done much better. This is just about the only recreation and social life that we get.

These characterizations represent common experiences of church members who find in the church an opportunity to participate in activities according to their interests, to do worthwhile church work, and to feel that they are loved and wanted by the other members.

The church helps adjust to the death of one's spouse

A man and wife usually become so thoroughly wedded that they work out a single life pattern during their married life. As a result, a severe crisis is prevented when one must adjust to the loss of the other. Havighurst often heard older persons in his research say,

"'I hope when my wife [husband] dies I can go too. Life won't be worthwhile after that.' This expresses the fear that man or woman has, after living forty or fifty years with a marital partner, of having to face life without the partner."[6]

This is an important problem of old age and one to which the church makes noteworthy contributions. Foremost among these is the love and comfort given to the bereaved church member by church leaders and other members. In addition to this, a certain alleviation of anguish and sadness is experienced by the church member who believes in an after-life; he realizes that death is not the end and that he may be united in the hereafter with his mate. These and other phenomena tend to make the adjustment to death of one's spouse easier for the church member. The following materials were selected to emphasize those items which were of obvious importance with respect to the problem of adjusting to the death of one's spouse.

A widow, living with her daughter in a two-room apartment, described how the church had aided her at the time of her husband's death.

I have been living here with my daughter for the past ten years, ever since my husband passed away. Although I had never been very active in the church, it was such a comfort to me at the time of my loss of my husband. There were several times when I just didn't know if I could stand it all by myself.

6. Robert J. Havighurst, "Old Age — An American Problem," *Journal of Gerontology*, 4:298-304, Oct., 1949.

Without the support of my religious beliefs and the church, I don't think that I would have made it.

Another widow described how at the death of her husband she turned to the church for companionship when she didn't find it anywhere else.

The church has meant a great deal to me during my life. I was brought up by an Auntie and she was very religious so I never knew anything but this way of life. This was so important to me when my husband died in his office suddenly one day. I fell back upon the church teachings but went elsewhere to find companionship which I did not find. I went to live with a dear lady but I didn't care for her friends and just couldn't seem to get to know them well. I went back to the church because that is where I first met my dear husband. They were so nice to me and I have so many lovely friends.

These remarks typify how the church leader is able to lend reassurance and comfort by indirect means. Further, they stress the fact that the value of the religious experience in alleviating the sorrow of losing one's mate is enhanced by the fact that the church serves this same function in all crises all through life. The church is always there. The older individual naturally turns to it in time of trouble, having done so on many previous occasions.

A woman who had become maladjusted at the death of her husband, and who apparently had not yet made a proper adjustment, told how the church had aided her in meeting this problem.

I tell you I hate to pass on my feelings about how I felt when my husband died because when I think or talk about it I get all broken up inside. My husband was so kind and good with such high morals I find it hard to understand why the Lord took him away from me. He was sick with cancer and when he died [at this point she started to cry and put her face in her hands and kept it there for ten minutes or more. When she finished she went over and picked up a photograph of her husband and started to talk about him and cry once more. Finally, she gained control of herself and the interview was continued]. I lost control over myself when my husband died and this is my stumbling block. All through it all it was wonderful to belong to the church. There is no way to measure the loss but I know the only things that keep me going are my two granddaughters and the hope that I will see my husband again in the hereafter.

An elderly man who was living with his daughter replied to a question concerning the death of his wife in the following manner:

My wife died in 1937; she died right here. She was a member of the church and did everything she could to be a good member. Anybody who has love in their hearts has love for their loved ones and if they are worthy they will have them in the next life.

A widower, eighty years of age, remarked that he was looking forward to the day of death because it would be a day of rejoicing in that he would be united with his family once again.

I have no fear of death; it can come any day to me. It is only a change over from death to life. I am the last of the family and am looking forward to meeting all those who have gone on before me and especially my wife who was taken many years ago. It was such a blessing to me to belong to the church at this time. The brothers and sisters were so kind and they did everything to make it less difficult for me in my bereavement.

A widow who felt that she was very close to death and ready to go declared her appreciation for all the fine men and women in the church who came to her aid when her husband died.

The church has meant everything to me and it helps me over everything. It gave so much comfort to me, and I know that the church is the biggest part of our lives. When my boys died, they came over and stayed with me and this helped me a great deal. When my husband died they came over and stayed all night. It makes me feel good when these men of the Lord come to the house. They don't come too often for me.

These few cases illustrate the value of the church to the member in meeting the problem of loss of spouse. The most frequently mentioned factors generally were the following. First, the church furnishes comfort and reassures the member that death is not the end. Next, comfort and service are given by the members of the church. Especially noteworthy was appreciation for the visits and reassurance given by church leaders who, in some instances, would come in pairs and spend the night after the husband or wife passed away. Nearly all subjects mentioned how much the nearness of their church leader or pastor meant to them at this time and how they appreciated his service. Much stress was also given to the comfort and love that always came from the other members who were in fact brothers and sisters in time of need. Third, the church furnished them with something constructive to do with time which was previously taken up with the deceased husband or wife. There were other areas in which the church aided the person to meet the problem of loss of spouse, but these were those most frequently mentioned.

THE CHURCH GIVES SUPPORT IN DARK DAYS AND CRISES

Throughout the ages the church has furnished comfort and reassurance to its members in days of discouragement and times of crisis. The illustrative materials which follow depict a few of the important ways the church performs this function.

A man who holds a doctor's degree mentioned how prayer often helped him to meet the problems of life.

> The church has helped me many times when I have had no other place to turn. There is always prayer when you are in trouble. I have several times asked them over at the church to pray for me to attain some goal or office, or to help me in time of need. This has helped me so many times, and they especially make an effort to reach out and try to help you as much as they can. I am just as sure of it as I am alive that the church and the teachings have helped me meet obstacles and serious problems during my life.

A married man, afflicted with a severe case of arthritis, disclosed how the church and its teachings had come to his aid and helped him meet his problem.

> I don't know what I would have done without this only comfort. There was the satisfaction of opening my heart to God in prayer. When a person is real sick and suffering so much that he cannot endure it and is in tears because of the pain, the suffering becomes light and others around you feel it more than you do. When the burden is lifted, it is beyond description how wonderful it is to know that God has done this for you. I have gone through seven operations and I have entered the operation room happily. Whether I lived through it or not, I would be perfectly contented. When I would come to after the operation, the nurses around would be in tears but I would wake up in smiles and they couldn't understand because I went under with security as I was satisfied knowing that God would take care of me. I have always loved the Lord and he has blessed me. I have gone to work at times when I would be grunting in pain and weak in faint and come home better. I always think of the Bible wherein it says, "As thy days are, thy strength shall be, and ye shall press on."

A business man mentioned that his church connections had helped him meet a financial crisis that nearly ruined him:

> During the depression I lost everything that I had, which amounted to a financial loss of about $40,000. I was completely ruined and it was only through the comfort that I received from the church that I was able to regain any sense of balance.

This man also relied on the church and his religious beliefs in meeting other problems which befell his family.

I lost a daughter some two years ago, and she was really an outstanding girl and meant so much to me. She had a stroke which paralyzed the left side of her body and she could not move her leg and arm. Through prayer she regained use of her leg but never the arm. Seeing her suffer made you wonder why a girl this age ought to have this affliction. It was God's will and not ours. Not long after she had another stroke and passed away. We know the Lord took her so that she would not suffer any more, and this knowledge made her loss much easier for us to accept. Grandma lived here with us for a time and our prayers were that she would not suffer from her tumor and our prayers were answered because she passed away in her sleep. This helped relieve the anguish of her loss and made us so close to God. Everyone prays when they find themselves in trouble and I can prove this as I have many atheist friends who do pray and turn to the Lord in times of trouble because this is the only thing that we can do sometimes.

This case represents an attitude prevalent among church members who feel that there are times when only God can offer comfort and reassurance to His sons and daughters. They believe this is so even among non-church members and atheists, as is indicated in the last statement of this man. It was said that during World War II there were no atheists in fox holes. Such remarks support the widespread belief that there comes a time when man is incapable of meeting his problems without the support of his Father in Heaven and naturally turns to the church or to religion to alleviate his conditions.

A lady described how the Lord had intervened in helping her in times of crisis because she had lived a good Christian life.

If you are close to the Lord you can work over any trouble that you will ever have in this life. I was a widow for 18 years and one time in San Francisco, California, I lost everything I owned and had a very bad time for a long time, but it never bothered me because I was close to God and He helped me. Another time when my husband and I were having a hard time I was hungry and we didn't have anything to eat although my husband had just found a job in a shipyard. I took a basket and started to the market although I didn't have any money and on the way I saw a gold piece in the street and there was no one around. God said it was mine and I said, "Thank you God." Just then a car came by and ran over it but when it had passed by the gold piece was still there and I came home with a basket of groceries all because the Lord had told me to go to the market. So many times I have been taken care of like that because I laid my hand in that of the Lord. If people

would only have faith because they don't get anywhere without
it. Yes, I know what the Lord can do in times of trouble. He
has healed me many times and I wouldn't be here today if I
was not spiritually close to God and close to the church.

Another man told how the Lord had blessed him many times
and similarly had been helped over the dark days of the depression. He spoke as follows:

Whenever I have been in a bad fix, the Lord has always come
to my aid. When I was in such financial trouble during the
depression, I asked the Lord to help me and He did. The man
who had my mortgage said to me that because I was a good
Christian he was going to make it easy for me. I owed $12,000
or more and it was past due, but he called me in and said that
he was going to cut down the payments and the interest almost
one-half. The Lord had blessed me because I tried to be a good
church member and kept close to Him at all times.

A married woman told how, upon meeting a crisis, her and
her husband's first thoughts were to turn to the church.

When our daughter was to be operated on for a serious condition our first thought was to contact our church leader so we
all could pray together. This was the only thing that we could
do, and it never failed us during our time of need. When our
camp was short of candidates, we were threatened with financial
ruin. We went into our bedroom and read and prayed and it
was like throwing a net into the waters because calls came in
faster than we could use them. We know that this was the
Lord blessing us because we have been good Christians and have
tried to help out over at the church. Whenever they need our
station wagons for parties or outings, we freely give because they
are the Lord's.

A married woman living with her husband in a private home
said the church had aided her on many occasions.

We have always turned to the church in time of trouble and
crisis in our family, and it has never failed to help when all
other means have seemed in vain. I'd hate to think what we
would do without the church, as there would be a void in our
lives without it. I have been healed many times by the Lord
and know of many persons who have also been healed and com-
forted by the spirit of the Lord. It has helped us through
business undertakings and problems of all types. We always meet
our difficulties with prayer and always receive an answer.

A married man who had been a member for forty years
indicated that the church helps one over the rough times in
life and alleviates tension by presenting hope for a brighter
tomorrow. He said:

Naturally a person going to church will meet his problems
and crises better than will the non-church person. The member

will have a better outlook on life in general. I imagine it would be terrible to be without religion. It gives you peace of mind because it answers a hope for the future. This is America's only hope in this time of crisis — to turn back to faith and religion. Unless we do, we are doomed. It has answered a lot of questions many people fret and stew about because it gives you a hope for a brighter tomorrow.

A single woman, living alone in a small apartment with her father, described her life as one crisis after another with the church being her only source of comfort.

It has not been easy for me to bear the troubles that have been mine since I came to America from Germany so many years ago. I have had to support both my father and myself. My life has been one problem after another, and sometimes I get so blue and unhappy I don't feel like living any more and then I remember the church and its teachings. Everything that I am and what I am doing is because of the church. I pray as I have been taught in the morning and at night and know that the Lord does watch over me and my father. The church has meant so much to me and helped me so much in everything.

An elderly lady who had never married and was living alone in a small apartment told how church members always cheered her up when she was in trouble or felt bad.

All I have to do is go there and they cheer me up, and this is so nice since mother is gone and can't aid me. Whenever I have any problems, the brethren from the church come right over and take care of them for me. I'm so thankful to the Lord for the church because it has helped me so many times in my life.

In this case, as in many others, the value of the church stems directly from the aid and comfort that comes from other members, contrary to the frequently reported reliance on church teachings and doctrines alone in meeting a given problem.

Another woman spoke of similar experiences in which the church had been a comfort in time of need because of the presence and reassurance of church leaders.

Any difficult problems that we or any members of our family have had, the church helps us over them. No matter when we have called on the church, they respond.

A man told how the church had aided him when he faced the most acute crisis of his life, bereavement.

The church has been a consolation on everything that has ever happened to me. My son's death is a good example. When he died, I didn't know if I would ever be able to pull myself together again, but when I realize that I will see him again, I am able to understand. Another time when the church helped me was when I was in a coal mine explosion. As I lay there in the dark not expecting to be rescued it was a great consolation to know that I had been baptized a member of the church. Without this knowledge, I believe I might have gone mad. The Gospel has similarly helped me over every problem and crisis that I have encountered during my life.

One last case similarly reveals how church experience is a comfort in time of family crisis.

When my daughter had a ruptured appendix and when my grandchild had pneumonia, we all got down in family prayer to ask the Lord's blessings during our time of trouble. Our prayers were sure answered. The doctor said he had done all he could do for us and to go home and pray because we were in God's hands. It's a wonderful thing that He's blessing us and taking care of us. It has helped us to meet all our troubles. We have had so many troubles I can't remember all of them, but the Lord has helped us in every case.

These quotations indicate that the church does offer support and encouragement in dark days and times of crisis. We found evidence of this in crises stemming from death of loved ones, economic ruin, broken homes, sickness and chronic disability, and in discouraging days of life whose specific problems are too numerous to mention.

THE CHURCH COMES TO THE INDIVIDUAL IN NEED

A valuable contribution of the church to alleviating the problem of old age is the fact that the church leader and his co-workers will continue to be interested in and come to the aged person even though his relatives, friends and other associates sometimes will not. Though older people generally are victims of neglect in society, the church has a long tradition of ministering to the aged as well as to other members. When a member is unable to go to the church, the church goes to the individual, a process which contributes to the well-being of the older person.

The first case illustrating this behavior pattern concerns a man who is unable to go to church very often because of a physical condition.

I don't know what I would have done without the church, which has been my only comfort during these days. I used to go often but not of late for obvious reasons. We appreciate it when the church people come here to visit us, and we also get beautiful sermons on the radio which make up somewhat for our not being in church.

An elderly woman living with her brother and sister also had a physical condition that prevented her from going to church. She said:

> I get much personal satisfaction when the church workers come to see me or my brother. I am glad that I am a member because it gives me a better outlook on life. They have never forgotten me over at the church and always bring me some gift at Christmas time and Thanksgiving.

A lady who was an active member and who served as a church visitor had this to say:

> The church tries to visit all of the members and especially those who are unable to come out to services. Everyone likes to feel that he is somebody and that he is an interest to someone. We try not to neglect anyone.

A disabled woman disclosed how much she appreciated the visits from the church workers.

> The church visitors come here very regularly. I don't get to go often, and they come to see me. I had a stroke and it was so wonderful to have the members come to visit me. No one came to see me except the church people. I don't care whether they come to see me any more or not, but I do want the church people to come. They are the only ones who really care about me.

An elderly man tried to get to church every Sunday but found satisfaction in having the church members come and visit him. He said:

> I used to go visit the older members when I was younger, and so I know something of what it means to go visiting. I enjoy having them come and teach to me, because no matter how old we get, we can still learn something.

A woman who formerly went to church regularly but was forced to reduce her attendance by an operation disclosed how she enjoyed the visits of members of her church.

> I am not very active anymore. I used to go all the time but I had a serious operation and had to stop. I miss going to all of the church activities, but especially do I miss the choir because I belonged to it all my life. One thing that helps me are the church visitors and the visits of the leaders. This keeps me in close contact with the church and what is going on.

A man, physically unable to get about well, expressed what must be a common feeling among many older persons in the church:

> I have been sick all year and am just now feeling better. I haven't been out of the house since last September. I haven't had many visitors except one or two neighbors and a friend. The church people come regular, and this has meant an awful lot

to me. I haven't lived up to the Gospel like I know it, but I appreciate how wonderful the church has been since I became ill. The last case concerns a woman who said:

I fell down the cellar stairs and am unable to make the trip to the church. I do appreciate the brothers and sisters coming here to visit me. I also enjoy the church paper and the programs on Sunday morning. These and the Gospel and caring for my sister are all that I have to live for except for my son who comes to see me sometimes.

These cases point out a unique function of the church: it continues to serve even when the member is unable to continue in the church activities. Members appreciate this and are made happier by it.

THE CHURCH SATISFIES BASIC SOCIO-PSYCHOLOGICAL NEEDS OF THE OLDER PERSON

Church activities and the religious experience tend to satisfy such basic social and psychological needs of members as the need to belong, to be valued, and to be understood. The opportunities furnished by organized religion for satisfying needs of older people are manifold and cover a wide area. The church may give the older person a sense of usefulness which has been lost in other spheres of life and thus help him to retain a feeling of self-respect. The church experience, in addition, may alleviate feelings of loneliness and being unwanted which are so prevalent among older persons. The following excerpts from interviews and those in earlier sections of this chapter illustrate these behavior patterns as they occurred to members in the study group.

A male member found in the church an opportunity to serve his less fortunate fellowmen. This gave him much personal satisfaction:

My greatest happiness comes from going down skid row and working for the church. We go down and put on non-denominational services for those fellows. After a night there we come away uplifted knowing that we have done good for somebody.

A widow described the importance of her job in the church, which was to visit members who were unable to attend services. She said:

I am not able to do much of anything anymore because I have lost the sight in one eye, and the vision in the other is not too good. About all I have time for nowadays are my home duties and, of course, visits to the semi-invalids who are on my list who I go to visit often. This is my job, and because I'm old like they are, they love to have me come and visit with them. It's better to have a person your own age come to visit you, and that's why I have so much to do because I'm about the only older person able to make these visits.

A man recounting his experiences in the church told of the personal satisfaction he had gotten from being the Scout Master of the local troop.

My younger life was devoted to Boy Scout work. I was one of the first Scout Masters in Chicago, as I became one forty years ago. It was my troop who dedicated Mecinac Park, and my boys also went to the Eastland disaster where they buried the two youngsters whose parents were never found. You read about this in the papers some time back. One thing about my troop you can't say about the others is that none of my boys turned out bad. They still come to me to get advice on Scout problems as I am a Scout official yet with probably the most experience of any Scout man in Chicago.

This man, like the first individual cited in this section, received a feeling of satisfaction and of self-importance in knowing that he was able to be useful in giving advice in a field in which he was highly qualified.

A married woman spoke concerning her usefulness in working for the poor and needy.

I have a lot of experience with activities in the church. I have always been busy doing one thing or another, but it is always for a good cause. Right now we are sewing things for people who need them. It is more blessed to give than to receive, and besides you get the personal satisfaction that you are doing something for your fellowman. Too few of us have that spirit.

Another lady told of how much pleasure she derived from serving in the church and how it made her feel so good to know that she belonged to such a nice group.

The people in the church look upon me as one who makes elaborate plans for even the most minor function. Last night we had all of the teachers here, and I made a lot of fuss in making sandwiches even though they said they would not come if I made a fuss. I enjoyed this, and it is my biggest pleasure because they always make a fuss over how nice I prepare for everything.

An elderly man disclosed the satisfaction he got from mingling with the other members and how it kept him from getting lonesome now that he had so much free time.

I never feel lonesome because I always go to church, and I make it my business to mingle with the people. I don't force myself, but I get right in and mingle with them. O, how I love to meet people!

A married woman described her usefulness to the church in the following manner.

> I feel sometimes that I am really useful to the church. I know that I try very hard anyway. I have a class with the children in Primary and have had this job for three years, so I am performing a good service there, don't you believe? Whenever they have a dinner or anything, they always come to me, so I suppose that they appreciate me and that I am of some use to the church.

A man who had been a member all his life told how he found satisfaction for his every need in the church.

> I have tried to live a good clean life and know that the Lord has blessed me way beyond my worth. I love the church and can testify to you that it is the most important thing in this life. It satisfies every need, and many times when I could not turn to my friends or even to my immediate family I have found love and kindness in the church. It has made me what I am today. I have worked with the boys for years and this has influenced my life so much. No, I could never be lonely with all my friends in the church and with all the boys who come to see me all the time. You see, if you do something good for a person he never forgets it, and these boys all remember me.

These illustrative materials depict some of the ways church experience helps to satisfy the need to belong, the need to be valued, and the need for a sense of usefulness which many times has been lost in other domains of life. It also tends to overcome feelings of loneliness which are so prevalent among older persons.

SUMMARY

The analyses in this chapter have shown that the church performs a valuable function in alleviating problems of old age and contributes to good personal adjustment. The interview data disclosed that church experience plays an important role in the alleviation of anxiety and fear concerning death through a provision of comfort and reassurance. Concerning this, it was found that the church member's fear of death was diminished through belief in an after-life which is fostered by the church's teachings.

The church offers to the individual an opportunity to participate in an atmosphere that is conducive to finding companionship and to continuing friendships when they are sometimes ended in other spheres. A significant finding was that the church provides activities and opportunities for its members to participate in a social environment in which the older person is welcome, which is not necessarily the case in other community institutions.

These cases have illustrated how the church helps in making adjustment to death of ones' spouse and to other crises of life. An aged person's relationship continues in the church after the time of retirement, physical disability, or old age even though associations with friends, co-workers and relatives sometimes do not. When he no longer is able to go to church, the church comes to him. Church experiences help to satisfy some of the basic social and psychological needs of members, such as the need to be loved, to belong, and to be useful. Finally, they also tend to minimize feelings of loneliness which are so common among older persons.

The significant conclusion of this chapter is that the church does perform a valuable function in alleviating problems of the older member. In doing so it contributes to good personal adjustment in old age.

CHAPTER 7

PROBLEMS OF THE OLDER PERSON IN THE CHURCH

VARIOUS WRITERS HAVE SUGGESTED that the aged have lost or
are in the process of losing their share of control in the various
social institutions. Ralph Barton Perry, for one, suggests that
the status of old people has reached an all-time low in that
youth has no respect for their authority and wisdom. He
notes that old people who are retired from business, the professions, politics and the army, do not in general command the
respect that old people have received in the past.[1] Other in-
vestigators, in contrast, have found that older people have not
been losing out to the extent that is generally believed and
that advanced age is not a deterrent to one's progress and
position.[2]

It would be expected that many of the behavior patterns expressed in the society at large will be carried over into the
church. Therefore, even in the church which holds the aged
in high esteem, we might find conflict between the aged person's conception of his role and the role of the younger member. Furthermore, it may be anticipated that the older person
in the church would bring with him tensions and anxieties
experienced in other spheres of life and would direct some
of his hostility toward fellow church members.

One source of possible dissatisfaction is a tendency for the
aged person to feel that he is being pushed aside by younger
members and that he is no longer wanted in the church. Another source of conflict that may arise is that the older person
may conceive of himself as the backbone and strength of the
church and feel that the younger member who is pushing him

1. Ralph Barton Perry, *Plea for an Age Movement*, Vanguard Press,
1942.
2. For example, see Otto Pollak, "Discrimination against Older Workers in Industry," *American Journal of Sociology*, 50:99-106, Sept., 1944.

aside lacks the maturity necessary to provide proper and adequate leadership.

Additional problems may lessen the value of the church experience to the older person. Some may stay away from church, or feel ill at ease if they do come, because they are unable to dress properly. Some may miss going because they are unable to contribute to the church as they have in the past due to reduced income which is typical of old age.

Others may be dissatisfied with changes that have taken place in the church framework and desire the old ways. Conflict may arise if the younger members feel that the aged are old-fashioned and set in their ways and as such block progress and change to newer and better things. The elderly may sense and resent these attitudes of the younger members, find it difficult to cooperate with them and consequently stay away from church. Finally, the older member may feel that he is being squeezed out of his position in the church by younger members and may not, as a result, feel as secure and close to the church as he would if this were not the case.

In summary, church experience may negatively affect successful aging by a number of conditions. Attention is now turned to case study descriptions of these and of circumstances which have brought them about.

SOME OLDER PERSONS FEEL THAT THEY ARE BEING PUSHED ASIDE BY YOUNGER MEMBERS

The first factor to be considered is the feeling of many older members that they are being pushed aside by younger members in the church.

The first case concerns a woman who was trying her best to do well at her church job because they would not, as she said, squeeze her out as long as she was efficient.

I sometimes feel that I am excess baggage over at the church and know of other older persons who feel the same way. I am surprised how many older people get squeezed out of their positions in the church and it bothers me to no end. They won't squeeze us out if we are efficient, and I work very hard so that they won't feel that I can't do my job any more.

The second statement, made by a male member, points out that this problem is present in his church and that sometimes the church appears cold and cruel to the older members.

This problem of older persons being pushed out of their jobs in the church is a critical area and much more extensive than is

generally believed. A well-run church has a program for both
the young and old members. We have this problem in our
church where they are so interested in the younger people that
they are always pushing us older members aside. Just recently
they made us move into the auditorium to make more room for
the younger members. I know that this made quite a few of the
old timers quite upset. Sometimes the church does not encourage us to come, and the church is even cold and cruel at times.

A woman mentioned how it was terrible to be pushed aside
in the church or any place else. She said:

Yes, I know that older persons are squeezed out in the church.
Just what do you expect me to think of this idea, young man?
It's terrible at church or any place.

An elderly man stated that he knew of many older persons
who had been eliminated from jobs in the church and stayed
home on that account.

I know many older persons who have been pushed off their
jobs and then have been squeezed out of their positions in the
church on account of their age. Not me though, because they
treat me nice, and young fellows treat me nice too. No one has
ever made me feel unwanted.

These remarks suggest that some persons either imagine or actually experience the phenomenon of being ejected from their
position in the church. Perhaps those who express such experiences are unduly sensitive because of frustrations and re-
buffs encountered in other spheres and are projecting their
afflictions to the church.

A lady member told how one of her friends had been deeply
hurt when he was forced out of his job in the church because
of his age. She said:

This problem of older members getting pushed out of their
jobs in the church is one of the problems we have at our church.
They are continually saying that we ought to put in the young
blood and to get rid of the old. They don't realize that they
need old blood in there running things. The Elders, for instance,
should be the most mature Christians. Some of our people are
not mature, and yet they take over the jobs. We should be able
to look up at an Elder when we need help and get the benefit
of his years of experience in the church. A dear friend of mine
was hurt because of the way they put him out of his church job,
which incidentally was about the only thing he had to take up
his time during the day. They changed the by-laws to state that
you could not serve more than two years. They make exceptions
for the young members but not for the old ones. They were
put out just because they are old. One of them was told that
he was on old fogy and this made him feel so bad he resigned.

The subject's friend had been pushed aside by a change in the by-laws which would limit the time served as a church Elder to a period of two years. Other subjects mentioned that the reason this by-law was changed was not to push the elderly out of their church jobs but to give more persons an opportunity to serve on church councils. These interviews were made just after this by-law had taken effect. It was obvious that the change was not appreciated by many older members who had been in office for many years.

An elderly man, who had been a member of the church for fifty years, claimed that some members were being neglected at the church and were staying home because of this.

> I am getting older and I have been a member of the church for a long, long time. There have been quite a lot of our older members leave the church on account of they are dissatisfied. They have left the church and will never come again except on Christmas and Easter. The two most important reasons for this trouble is that we get put out of office and because .... passes up the older ones and mingles with the younger. One man and wife in my pew don't come because they feel they are neglected. He shakes hands with us older people but we are not respected. All we do is go and listen to the sermons.

This man was one of those who had experienced being put out of office because of the changed by-laws. He felt that he was neglected by the church leaders in favor of the younger members and that all that remained for him was to listen to the sermons. In a further statement he remarked that he had contributed financially to that church for years, that it was as much his as anyone else's, and that he could not see why he was not wanted.

A woman member told of how her father was affected when he was put out of his church job after having served, according to her, for fifty years.

> It's a terrible mistake to squeeze the older persons out of their church jobs. They don't seem to realize how much those jobs mean to them when they get older and can't do much of anything else. My father was an Elder since I was two. Just last year they put him out. It just about crushed my father. Though he isn't as active as he used to be, they at least should have given him a less active job. It aged my father quicker and took his last interest. He was retired and his only interest was the church, and when they took that, he had no further interest.

A male member told how he had been slighted at the church He said some of the older members stayed away rather than be treated that way.

There is more conflict in the church than there used to be. It used to be that the younger people were more obedient and ready to be led. Today they want to take over and lead the older people. They do this in the church. It shouldn't be so, but I know this is the case. Still they don't stop to think about the older person. They feel that a man of fifty is not capable of holding up his end of it, and I think he is better because he has had experience and is holding firm. You can't stop being a human being when you go to church, and it's that way on the outside. Nature will take its course because people don't stop to think. Sure, some of the older persons are staying home because they feel they have been slighted and don't like the way certain churches are being governed and their little say-so doesn't matter much. They stay away rather than be embarrassed because of the way they have been treated.

Another case concerns a woman who didn't fit into the church as she had when she was younger.

There is a clique over at the church now and it's hard to get to talk to them, let alone be loved by them. They stick together and they don't invite you in. I like the way the church used to be when it was like a family there. You used to know you were welcome and you would help one another. Now they are not concerned with your troubles, but they are just hard subjects which we can't always understand. It used to be that we knew everybody and they knew us and missed us when we were not there. Now they don't seem to care. They are not very friendly here now. They sometimes go right by you and don't pay any attention to you. It's just a few that shake hands with you; they usually shake hands with the younger members. This doesn't make me feel very good. I sometimes feel lonely and feel like running right out the front door.

A summary description of how older persons feel when they think the younger members believe them to be "old fogies" and are pushing them aside is taken from the remarks of an elderly woman who concluded:

One thing I would like to say is that no matter what anybody says or does, they ought to remember that the older a person is, the more religion they have in them. I know an old lady who died of a broken heart and no one cared for her. The church doesn't care for its old people like they used to. We need a home here. They do cater an awful lot to the young to keep them in the church, but they look on us as old fogies who are useless. The old persons are pushed aside as they have lived their lives and are no longer useful. They keep after the young because they have money and they don't want them to mix with the other denominations. I think old people will keep coming out as long as they are able to, no matter what they do at the church. It's to be expected that older people are better and more religious. Younger people need more life. They just ignore the old people and cater to the young people. They know we won't leave the church, so they give all the attention to the younger members.

This lady had lived her whole life in the church and now felt that she was being treated discourteously to make room for younger members.

From the foregoing statements it is evident that many older persons in the church either are being neglected in favor of the younger members or imagine that they are. Others report being dismissed from jobs, which apparently has an unhealthy effect on older members and causes embarrassment, or as reported by one subject, "crushing" the individual. Whatever the causes, real or fanciful, it is evident that some oldsters have these experiences and it appears that the condition is not favorable to good adjustment in old age.

SOME OLDER MEMBERS STAY AWAY BECAUSE THEY ARE UNABLE TO CONTRIBUTE FINANCIALLY

Another factor that may tend to keep the aged from feeling secure in and attending church is their inability to continue to contribute financially to it. A large proportion of older people have to adjust to reduced incomes, and many cannot afford to contribute as freely as was once possible.

A lady related that she would make every sacrifice to contribute to her church and that if she were unable to do this, she would not attend. She said:

Yes, if I was not able to contribute to the church, it would bother me so that I wouldn't feel right if I were to attend. Although I don't account according to Hoyle, I have no use for members who don't contribute to the church. I'd do it if I had to cut my leg off or go without everything to pay it.

This member, in addition to pointing out that she would not attend if she were unable to contribute financially, reveals an attitude toward persons who are unable to contribute that may well be a source of difficulty. It is very likely that such views are shared by others and felt keenly by those unable to pay.

A man who made it plain that he wouldn't stay away under any conditions went on to tell of the importance of money in the church.

I wouldn't stay away from church under any circumstances, including not being able to pay my pledge. I do know that they value the attendance of the old people by the amount of money they donate. I've been around enough to know that they **do** ease the poor ones out.

Another lady said that she knew some old people who stayed away because they didn't have funds to give to the church.

No, I wouldn't stay away, I've given so much all my life, but I would be embarrassed if I couldn't. There are a lot of people who stay away, even though they shouldn't, for this reason. They use this as an excuse to stay away.

It is significant to note that even though this lady believed it wrong to stay home because of lack of funds, she stated that she would be embarrassed if she were not able to give to the church.

A retired male member said that he would stay home and gave a typical reason why he would do so.

You know I gave my first twenty-five dollars to the church, but I would stay home if I couldn't pay up now. I would because they don't pay any attention to those who don't pay.

A widow, sixty-five years of age, told how she had stopped going to church because of money matters.

Money shouldn't matter in the church, but it does. I stayed home because I was offended because they preached on how stingy we were with God. They don't know if we are or not. We might be starving, and they would never know. I give all I can which is different than when my husband was alive. Inflation or not, I don't get any more. I just felt so bad when I couldn't give that I felt I ought not to go so much until I was able to pay again.

An elderly man similarly replied that he would stay home because he would be getting something for nothing if he made no contribution.

I definitely wouldn't go as often, that is true. I would be getting something for nothing then, and that is not the way it should be. I am under obligation to support the church, and if I had any money, that is where it would go. Most churches have a struggle as it is.

Another statement came from a married woman who evidently experienced remorse because she didn't have funds to contribute to the church. While it had not kept her completely away, it did affect her attitude toward participating in the church.

I've seen certain people forgotten and overlooked in the church. It's like politics — those with money get attention and those without do not. In church people are just like they are any place else; there are always those who think they are better because they have more money. We get forty-three dollars each week after taxes and have to work hard for that. We can't do much with that. We can't contribute to buildings and all the other things. It makes us feel real bad, but we won't quit the church because the Lord knows our circumstances and He knows our situation and is our judge. But you must realize by now that your prestige in the church depends on how much money you have. I've got letters in my house right now asking me to contribute to the church. I just am not able to do this and don't know what to do about it. I don't believe in that stuff, but it doesn't change my mind about the Gospel.

These quotations indicate that being unable to contribute sometimes causes older persons to stay away from the church. In other cases the members continued to participate but experienced dissatisfactions because of their financial conditions. The effects of this problem are compounded because the older person has a difficult enough time adjusting to a reduced income in other areas of life.

We may conclude that lack of funds does sometimes cause persons to stay away from the church even though the Gospel through the ages has made no distinction between the rich and the poor.

SOME OLDER MEMBERS STAY AWAY BECAUSE THEY ARE UNABLE TO DRESS WELL

Coincidental with the many other problem areas of old age is the inability of many older persons to dress as well as they did when they were younger. Many times this is the result of reduced income, while other times it may be due to physical inability, general indifference or other reasons. Regardless of the cause, it is possible that this inability to dress well plays an important role in keeping older people away from the church. This is illustrated by the following cases.

A married man, who was well dressed when interviewed, charged that some churches don't encourage their members to come if they are not well-dressed.

Some churches don't encourage us to come if we are not dressed well. If we do come, we won't be welcome. It isn't like it should be or like it used to be. I remember out in Kansas when the old Civil War veterans with long beards were welcomed and they slept out in the open and came to church plenty dirty. I am against relegating old persons to oblivion. A poorly dressed person is given the cold shoulder at church by the members. It's a human tendency, and it's bad but very widespread.

From these remarks we gather that this practice may be widespread, for this man, having been a professional organist, had spent a lifetime visiting the various churches. It is significant that he stated that the poorly dressed person is given the cold shoulder by other members. Another older member directly stated that he himself had no use for those who didn't dress well.

> Put this down for me. Some have means to do it but are in a savings rut and tight. If they would appear more tidy the reaction wouldn't be to have them stay home. We leave them alone and they are overlooked if they are sloppy and dirty at church, and they ought to be.

A male member told that some of his friends in the church were staying home because they didn't have proper clothes to wear. He said:

> Do older people ever stay home from church because they can't dress as well as they did when they were younger? Yes, I know that they do because I know of some people in this church who stay at home because they can't dress so well.

A widow gave a new insight on this subject when she said that her problem was not that of not being able to dress well but that she couldn't dress to please the other members now that her husband was dead.

> I guess I could dress up more to go to church, but they just won't let me even though I would like to do it. Many times I have dressed up kind of gay, and they make fun of me and say, "She is trying to catch another husband," or "She has forgotten she is an old lady." I am just now wearing red, and I never like black because my husband didn't like black. They all think I ought to continue to wear black clothes and they don't know the reason why I don't, and it makes me feel so sad that I sometimes don't go.

This lady, sixty-five years of age, went on to make a significant statement: She said that she always liked to go over to a little social club because the members were so friendly and complimentary about one's appearance. This is especially noteworthy when it is considered that she sometimes stayed home from church because people would make fun of her clothes. She said:

> I just love to go with a friend of mine to a little women's group because the women are so friendly and complimentary about personal appearance. The other night I was nearly knocked off my chair. I wasn't dressed up even special and a friend said to me "............... you look so pretty." I said, "I haven't even a dime to offer you." This came right out of the blue sky. Some tell me my earrings are pretty and other nice things like that. I wish it was like this over at the church. But it isn't what is on

the outside that counts; it's what is on the inside that is important.

A woman stated that she thought the younger generation put too much stress on clothes and sometimes hurt the older ones who were not able to dress as well.

It's terrible how the younger generation only think of clothes. And when the older person forgets and begins to slip all over, it shows in his dress first of all. The young people just think of clothes and hurt many of these older persons by just snubbing them. It's a real shame, too.

Another woman told how this was not the situation at her church because it was stylish to dress up, and all the women were very well dressed.

Unless older people have children to tell them what to buy, they generally get in a rut. Some are poor and some don't feel the need to dress up. But women forty to sixty are the best dressed ones — better by far over the younger ones. Some cities and countries are better dressed than others. Our church is well dressed and stylish. Some poor women stay away because they can't keep up in dress, but we treat them all the same, so it isn't our fault. It's a subjective thing and up to the person.

Another woman mentioned that it is the people who are guilty and not the church.

Most people dress up in our church. I for one take pride like any woman and like to look presentable. I don't like to buy new things but I like them. If I could get someone to shop for me I'd love it. I haven't enough money to buy at a smart shop. If older members do stay home, it's their own fault. No church would let them stay away; it's like a doctor wouldn't let a patient die. I know a lady who didn't have the money to subscribe to the church magazine but subscribed to the *Reader's Digest*. It's a matter of mind. If you are enough of a Christian to want to do a job of keeping up, you can. The church wouldn't make it noticeable. Not that the church is free, it has cost me a pretty penny all of my life. They might feel uncomfortable, but some person, some lady cat, may hurt the person but not the church.

A man, eighty years of age, said he thought that there was no excuse for an older person coming to church dirty or with ragged clothes and that they wouldn't feel good if they did come.

Some older people don't dress. You can be poor and still be clean. When old clothes are torn they can be patched and look good if clean. The trouble is that people let themselves go and don't care any more. They let themselves go and say why should I dress up? This makes the younger people mad sometimes.

These few remarks selected from the interview material illustrate the idea that some older persons stay away from church because they do not dress as well as they did when they were younger.

SOME OF THE AGING STAY AWAY FOR OTHER REASONS

In addition to the foregoing factors were other items which accounted for older persons' staying away from church. The illustrations presented in this section were secured in answer to a question addressed to the subjects asking them why, besides the reasons already given, oldsters tend to stay way from the church.

(1) Some felt neglected or slighted for reasons besides those mentioned earlier.

The first case is that of an older man who disclosed that some stay away because they believe that they are not appreciated.

> I know of some older members who are sensitive and think they are not noticed and appreciated. Because of this, they are not satisfied today. I know how this is, because I've been this way all of my life, but it isn't good enough. These people think they are doing as well as they can but are not appreciated, so they stay home.

A similar statement came from a married woman. She said:

> For one thing, older persons stay away because they have lost vision and interest. Also they feel neglected. They are not really, but they feel that they are neglected and because of this some stay home.

This idea that some older members were staying away from church because they felt neglected was further stressed by a male member.

> I know of a man and wife in my pew who don't come any more because they are neglected. He shakes hands with us older people, but we are not respected.

A lady member in agreement with the foregoing said that many older persons stay home because of neglect.

> Many older persons stay away from the church, even though they would like to attend, because their feelings are hurt when they are neglected. I think this is foolish because you only hurt yourself, but many of them do it anyhow.

A somewhat similar statement was given by another older lady member.

> Some of the old ones get offended and don't feel they are acquainted with the people. Because of this, they would rather stay away than come to church.

A final statement comes from a woman member who says that many oldsters stay away because they have been disregarded.

> Many stay home because they have been slighted and don't like the way certain churches are being governed, and their little say-so doesn't matter much, and they stay away rather than be embarrassed because of the way they have been treated.

These few cases might be supplemented by others from interview records. They are sufficient to make it clear that at least some older persons stay away from the church because they feel neglected or slighted.

(2) Many older people are kept away from church because they are not able to get transportation for one reason or another. The following excerpts from the case materials illustrate this factor.

A widower living with his sister related the following reason why he felt some oldsters were staying home from church.

> I suppose it is quite a chore for a lot of older people to get ready and to come to church. Most of them live a long ways away from the church and can't get transportation. I know several that way. It's a hard job to get to the church.

A similar instance of staying away because of lack of transportation is depicted by a woman member.

> One of the most important reasons why old persons stay away from church and other activities is because they do not have adequate transportation. They usually do not drive their own automobiles and are seldom able to ride the street cars and buses.

Another woman reported somewhat the same situation when she said:

> I believe that some old ones stay away because they put too much work on them, and then again they just can't come out because they don't have transportation.

These few cases point out that the lack of transportation does contribute to keeping the aging away from church in many instances.

It was indicated earlier that inability to contribute financially to the church because of reduced income was one of the factors which kept many older persons from attending. Another closely related item is that many older persons are unable to pay the transportation charges without disrupting their budgets. While this may appear trivial to the average person who has not experienced the loss of income, it nevertheless is a real problem for numerous older persons, as the following materials demonstrate.

A widow living alone related the following:

> Many older people stop going to church because it is hard to get there and especially when the weather is bad and rough. Another reason is that it costs thirty cents, and I have to figure these thirty cents, and I stay home on account of this many times. Because of this I am going to change to a church which is on the corner.

Here we note a concrete example of a member staying home from church because she could not afford the thirty cents necessary to make the trip each Sunday.

Other persons reported comparable experiences. An elderly woman living just a short distance from church said:

> Both my husband and myself have a hard time getting out to church because of difficulty in getting there. Although we seldom miss we find that it is quite expensive in making the round trip. We appreciate it when we get a ride with other members.

An older woman who had never married and was living alone said:

> Some people don't come to church because they don't feel so good. We ought to visit them more. Carfare is an awful lot. I don't get much pension, and I have to give some to the church. If they could arrange some way to get us there. I have a few people who drive me home. They should try to give us older ones a lift or arrange to have a bus or something.

A final case is that of an elderly member who spoke of the expense involved in getting to church.

> One does everything he can to go to church if he is close, but thirty-four cents is too much for going on the car. When it was five cents it wasn't so bad, but it costs too much now. I've tried to walk it, but I get so tired that I just can't do that very often.

Here was a man of eighty years trying to walk ten blocks or more to church because he did not have the thirty-four cents to pay his way on the streetcar. This case, which most likely is typical of many, exemplifies the pitiful condition wherein reduced incomes affect church attendance in old age.

(3) An increase in the extent and severity of physical illnesses is a common experience in later life. It was found to be another reason why older persons stay away from the church.

A man living with his sister spoke as follows:

> I used to go often but not of late for various reasons, the most important reason being my physical condition. We get our sermons mostly from the radio.

A woman told how the bad weather affected her so that she couldn't attend regularly.

It is hard for me to go when it is cold or when I get my feet wet, so I have to stay home on many occasions.

A widow, living with her daughter, spoke of some of her friends who were physically unable to attend church.

I have a number of friends who are very lonesome and I am trying to get them to come to the church, but most are too physically ill to go.

An ardent member told how his poor health kept him from going to church on many occasions.

I love to go to church, but sometimes I just can't make it because of my poor health. When I am able I never miss, but sometimes I can't help myself and have to miss.

A woman member said:

I get sick if I go out too much and I stay home because of this quite often. There must be many old ones who just can't come out physically.

Another woman member spoke as follows:

Some old people don't feel good, so they stay home where they can read their church books and observe the Sabbath day.

These few remarks illustrate clearly that poor health and physical conditions keep many older members from attending regularly, as would be expected.

The illustrative interview materials in this section have uncovered several factors besides those previously discussed which account for many older members' staying away from the church. First, it was disclosed that many oldsters stay away from the church because they feel neglected or slighted by the other members when they do come. Further, it was found that lack of transportation played an important role in keeping many oldsters from church. Another item closely related to the lack of transportation was the high cost of transportation which many were unable to pay because of reduced income. Finally, it was disclosed that physical illnesses played a major role in keeping many older members from attending regularly.

MANY OLDER MEMBERS ARE DISSATISFIED WITH CHANGES IN THE CHURCH

One of the foremost adjustment problems of oldsters as observed by specialists is an inability to adjust to changed conditions. In agreement with these observations, it was found that many older persons were discontent with changes that had taken place in the church and that they longed for the old ways which they believed were better.

The first case is an elderly man who spoke as follows:

Frankly, the church is not as good as it used to be. There are too many people with new ideas that are not good for the church.

A married woman said:

I have a hard time slipping into the women's activities because they have odd ideas. Although my interests have always been in the choir and Sunday school, it isn't the same anymore. The choir is best, but the other organizations are trying to change too fast. It is very different than when my dad was alive. People don't realize what they are doing, or else they don't pay attention.

Another woman expressed a common feeling among many older persons in the following statement:

I don't mind the new ideas they bring into the church if they are good, but for the most part they are not and they only lead to confusion for all concerned. The old methods are objective and there is no sense in changing.

A man who had been a member of the church since 1918 mentioned one specific change which was particularly bothersome to him.

I'm glad you asked about change. I have traveled around quite a bit. It surely is sad how they have changed things over at the church. People of late, and I've grown up to see it happen, are in a more nervous state. When you are nervous you want to hurry up and to change everything. Naturally it doesn't get you any place but they keep on changing things. Haste makes waste and they do this at the church.

A woman member made a brief and concise statement when she said,

The old way is the best way.

A male member declared that he stayed home because things are not like they used to be in the church.

The younger people are too smart for one thing. They know it all. If you can't make them change their minds, they run wild with new ideas. The kids in church don't have sense to speak to you. They ruin our church. We never allowed all this when I was younger. That is a house of God, and it ought to be like it used to be a long time ago. Many of us stay home now because it isn't.

Whether or not this member actually experiences such behavior or is merely projecting his own shortcomings to the church is not discernable. However, this exemplifies an inability to adjust to change and manifests itself in his being so disturbed that he would rather stay at home.

Another member indicated somewhat the same attitude toward certain changes that had taken place in the church.

There are certain changes that have occurred in the church which have resulted in bad results which are very ɪ oticeable.

There have been too many changes made along this line. For instance, I bought this place, and some of the tenants living here were invited by my folks to go to church with us. On several occasions they have accompanied them to church dances and meetings. Now they don't wish to go to any of the meetings because there is no reverence in the church. It didn't used to be this way and I wish they would change back again.

Another lady stated that the church was getting too complex:

The church is getting too complicated today. I'd like to go back to the old ways. The Gospel and the church are okay, but there are too many complications today.

From these cases we see that many of the elderly are displeased with changes that have taken place in the church. This has resulted in negative attitudes on the part of older persons, which range from general dissatisfactions to ceased attendance. It is evident that some oldsters lack the ability to adjust to changed conditions in the church and, as a result, are quite dissatisfied with present conditions.

CONFLICT OFTEN EXISTS REGARDING THE ROLE OF THE OLDER PERSON IN THE CHURCH

The final factor which was found to influence attitudes of the older members was a conflict which exists between the younger and older members regarding the role of the older person in the church. The following cases, in addition to those in the first section, illustrate this behavior.

An elderly lady did not voice her opinions on vital matters at the church because she felt younger members thought that the older ones were old fogies.

I often keep quiet when they discuss things over at the church because the younger ones don't have much respect for we older one's opinions. They think we are old fogies and has-beens.

Another woman voiced somewhat the same view when she said:

They call us old crabs whenever we try to say anything about the way things ought to be at the church.

Still another woman spoke as follows:

Yes, some are put out just because they are old. One of the things they told them was that they were old fogies and they railroaded the young ones in office. Because they said the old ones were old fogies, this made them feel bad so they resigned.

These remarks reveal something concerning the attitude of older members with respect to their relations with younger members in the church. Here we see older members refusing to participate in church activities while others quit the church altogether because of the attitudes of younger members.

Generally the older members feel that there is a definite place for them in the church, as is expressed by an older man:

> I think old people can do much work in the church. There is a place for them. Some firms employ older persons and get along well with them, and these persons are good for years. For instance Toscanini is eighty-two and his conducting is superb. He is a master of music and has the most beautiful interpretation possible. This idea that younger people should replace older ones is all wrong.

Other older members stated that they believed that younger members were important in the church but that they should always be under the supervision and direction of older members who have more experience and knowledge and are in essence the backbone and strength of the church.

A simple pertinent statement came from a lady member when she said:

> We oldsters ought to be present to watch over the discussions of the younger members who lack wisdom and experience.

A woman believed some of the younger ones would like to take over, but the older people were better for nearly all positions in the church.

> Older men have more power and respect in the church and any place else, but the younger men are always trying to push them aside. The younger people push too much and try to dominate everything. Old ones are not too anxious like the younger people. They take the bull by the horns and push on. People want young people and young ideas, but older ones are better in nearly all positions in the church.

Another woman said that older members were better leaders because they had more religion in them.

> The older they are, the more religion they have in them. It is to be expected that older people are better and more religious. Younger people need more life and should wait their turn.

One man stated that it wasn't for anyone but the Lord to decide when the old ones should retire in favor of the younger members. He said:

> Today the young people want to take over and lead the older people. They do this in the church too. It shouldn't be so, but I know this is the case. Still they don't stop to think about the older person and how he has made the church what it is. They feel a man of fifty is not capable of holding up his end of it. I think he is better because he has had the experience and is holding firm. There should never be retirement in the church or any

place else. They should go on and on. Their wisdom makes up for their physical condition. As long as the Lord lets them live they should go on and on. Only the Lord should stop them and not anyone else.

A man who believed the younger members could neither do a good job nor were living as they should, spoke as follows:

They are not older people. I'm one and we are still young. I don't go to shows on Sunday and other things like that. We used to study our Bible on Sunday afternoons. We were never allowed to go to dances and shows on Sunday. My dad always said this was a day set by the Lord, and we observed it. We were good humble people in those days. That's what's wrong with people today. They don't care about the church, but they want to take over and push us good Christians aside, and they couldn't do a good job if they did take over.

This man brought out one significant difference between the younger and older members which probably is responsible for their conflict as much as anything else. This is that young people today have been brought up in a much different society from that in which the older members lived in their youth. Along with the shift from a rural to an urban type of living has come a similar shift from sacred to secular patterns of life. Younger people today generally do not experience the same need for respecting the Sabbath and church-going as did their elders who went to church as a family unit and seldom missed. This, of course, could be elaborated upon, but it suffices here to suggest that this is one source of the conflict between the younger and older members.

A final statement, given by a woman, reflects the feeling common among the elderly that there is a place for the younger person as long as the leadership is supplied mainly by older members.

The young ones should do many jobs in the church. Older people can do things well, but young ones bring in new ideas. My husband plays the organ and he is old. I like the young people in there working. Lots of times I thought, why do they give the older people jobs when the younger people could do it? They shouldn't take over altogether because the old have more wisdom and knowledge. Ever since I was in the church the older persons have held all the important jobs and that is the best way.

These quotations indicate the older members in the church sometimes experience dissatisfaction because they sense that younger members believe them to be "old fogies" and "has-beens" and are trying to take over their jobs. The aging not only resent this intrusion of young people into what they believe is their special sphere, but they also believe that they are capable of furnishing the basic leadership in the church. They believe that, because they are mature and have experience and knowledge, it is only right that they should supply the leadership necessary to conduct the affairs of the church. The foregoing quotations have shown that these older persons are very sensitive about this and have in some instances become so dissatisfied with the attitudes of younger members toward them that they have kept out of the church activities and sometimes quit the church altogether. This is another important area in which the older person experiences dissatisfactions in the church.

Summary of problems in church

The cases presented have shown that the circumstances which contribute to dissatisfactions experienced by older persons in the church are exceedingly varied. They have shown that older persons experience dissatisfactions in many areas in the church and that this, together with certain other factors incidental to old age, was responsible for many not being regular church attenders.

It was found that many of the aged feel that they are being neglected in favor of the younger members. Some reported being pushed out of church jobs because of their age. Others reported dissatisfactions and embarrassment because they are unable to contribute financially to the church as a result of reduced incomes typical in old age.

Some older persons were discontented and stayed away from the church because they couldn't afford to dress properly. Others reported staying away from the church and reflected general feelings of unhappiness because no matter how hard they tried, they were not appreciated by the younger members.

Another reason given for staying home was the lack of suitable transportation. Most found it too cumbersome to ride on public conveyances and either did not own an automobile or did not drive. Some older members, in addition, couldn't afford to pay the fare when they did choose to ride the bus or streetcar. Thirty cents each way puts a serious crimp in small budgets already skimpy due to inflation. Some also miss going to church because of physical illness.

According to the interview materials, many old people are dissatisfied with changes that have taken place in the church and unhappy with things as they are at the present time.

Finally, older persons sometimes experience dissatisfactions because they believe younger members imagine them to be "old fogies" and "has-beens" and are trying to take over their jobs in the church. The aged not only resent this, but many feel that they, because of their wisdom and experience, should supply the leadership for the church. This conflict was so severe that in at least a few cases members quit participating in certain church activities, and others stopped going to church entirely.

The significant conclusion which develops is that many old members are not getting all they possibly could from the church because they experience dissatisfactions in their relationships with the younger members and because of other factors stemming from old age.

CONCLUSION

The data in the foregoing three chapters — 5, 6, and 7 — are based upon experiences of older members in two large city churches. The conclusions are not limited to them, however, for many referred to friends and other own past experiences in other churches. In addition, every American church shares some characteristics with others. The discussion also dealt only with certain selected topics. Numerous additional adjustment values were suggested and more problem experiences were intimated in the interviews but are not emphasized in this report because they were not systematically analyzed in the research project upon which it is based. As a sociological study, emphasis was placed upon inter-personal relationships and socio-psychological problems and their impact upon the personal and social adjustment of the older person. Theological doctrine was not stressed in the analysis.

Among additional experiences in the church which promote personal adjustment are the assistance the church often gives in the midst of personal problems of health and disability, economic difficulties and social needs. The welcoming of all people into the church often helps to integrate older and younger persons into a common fellowship like that of an extended family which includes people of all ages. When the aging are treated as individuals who are a part of this larger fellowship, and not categorically as *old* people, the morale of the older member is greatly built up. Since the church is known to be a source of help in time of trouble and has been used that way in earlier crisis experiences of life, it often is called upon when emergencies arise in old age. This may be labeled by the skeptic as "ambulance service," but ambulances indeed are needed for people who are suffering from wounds inflicted in a world filled with problems. Churches that have programs of the kinds referred to in the next chapter to meet specific needs of the aged do a great deal to promote the adjustment of members and others who come under their influence.

The findings from this and the other studies being reported on in this book indicate that older persons have additional problems with respect to their relations with the church. Although these studies were not theologically oriented, it is apparent from their findings that theological beliefs often fall short of the ideal held by the church for them. Uncertainty about the resurrection, nagging doubts about the nature of the future life, beliefs that heaven is solely a reward for doing good, living a clean life or "making a grade," misquotations of the Bible which distorted its teachings, equating money and church attendance with godliness, and the idea that belief in an afterlife or a lack of fear of death is equivalent to faith in God and assures salvation seem to be implicit in certain of the interviews.

The problems of adjusting to changing ideas of right and wrong in the church as society changes and to social and cultural modifications which are a basis for generational conflict were not explored as thoroughly as they could be in future studies. The way in which physical health is related to such life-habits as over-eating has implications for the church and the practical ethics it teaches. The preference of a social club over the church because of different attitudes of members toward clothing, as well as unmet problems of transportation and other material needs were evident in some cases. A major problem implied for church leadership is how to keep the older members interested in the church with a continuing vision of their place of service and fellowship in it.

If the problems of older people in the church, the adjustment values they do experience, and those that could be provided in church for them are kept clearly in mind by church leaders, the church will be able to do far more for them than if it simply continues its traditional program with no special thought given to the peculiar needs of the various sub-groups represented within the congregation and the community. The suggestions in the following two chapters are not related item by item to the problems and adjustment values which have been indicated by these case studies. Their overall message is that the church should use that which is wholesome to best advantage and at the same time should try to overcome the problems often met by older people in the church. This implies simultaneous use of older persons in the church program, with the result, among others, that their personal adjustment will be enhanced as they are accepted by others and by themselves as having a useful role to play in the work of God through His church.

CHAPTER 8

WHAT THE CHURCH CAN DO FOR OLDER PEOPLE

OF ALL INSTITUTIONS in the typical American community, the church is the one in which older people are most apt to participate and hold membership. They are not usually expected to retire from it in the later years.[1] The church today ministers to the physical, social, and economic as well as the spiritual needs of man because of the recognition that all areas of life are intimately interrelated.

As we consider the role of the church in relation to older people, we must realize, of course, that every church is different from every other church. No two churches are identical in their membership composition, social and cultural traditions, environmental setting or administrative organization as it actually functions in dealing with practical details of its work. Some churches are in the country, others in the city, and still others in suburban areas; some are large while others are very small; some have a large number of well-educated lay leaders while others have none; some have many older people in the church and in the surrounding community, while others have few or none. Because of these and other variations, the suggestions that follow do not apply to all churches with equal force. What would work well in one church might be a complete failure in another. Hence there is a need for democratic evaluation of proposed programs by those who will take part in or be affected by them.

The suggestions in this chapter involve some of the activities possible by the church on behalf of older people. In the suc-

1. For a study of public opinion concerning the roles of older people, see Robert J. Havighurst and Ruth Albrecht, *Older People*, Longmans, Green and Co., 1953, Appendix A, pp. 343-364. See also Joseph T. Drake, "Some Factors Influencing Students' Attitudes Toward Older People," *Social Forces*, 35:266-271, Dec., 1956.

ceeding chapter, suggestions of things older people can do for the church are given. The overlap between these types of suggestions will be obvious to the careful reader; in actual practice in the local church no sharp distinction can be drawn between what the church can do for older people and what older people can do for the church. As the church helps older people, e.g., in a social or a recreational program, it will at the same time need the help of some older people in positions of leadership as well as in carrying out some of the routine activities that are necessary.

Not all of the suggestions given in these chapters come directly out of the findings of empirical studies; many of them are the products of a systematic study of current literature, some of the best and most directly pertinent of which is referred to in the footnotes. Others have come in the form of inferences and generalizations from news reports and from personal observations of the authors. Present evidence indicates that these suggestions are prudent, practical, and consistent with current social science knowledge, but no finality is intended by this listing. Rather, as is indicated in the appendix, these suggestions need additional testing and evaluation.

With this background, let us turn to some of the things the church can do to help meet the needs of older people that have been presented in earlier chapters of this book.[2]

2. An excellent source on special problems of older people in the church and what effective programs for them should involve is Elsie Thomas Culver, *New Church Programs with the Aging,* Association Press, 1961.
Valuable "how to do it" pamphlets to help churches and church groups face the problems and needs of older people are *The Congregation and the Older Adult* (Division of Welfare, National Lutheran Council, 1959) ; *Older Persons in the Church Program* (Board of Christian Education, Presbyterian Church in the U.S.A., 1957) ; H. Lee Jacobs, *Senior Citizens in the Church and Community* (Institute of Gerontology, State University of Iowa, 1960) ; *How to Serve Your Older Members* (Community Council of Portland, Oregon, n.d.) ; *Older Persons in the Church Program* (General Conference Mennonite Church, Newton, Kansas, 1960), and the Lutheran Laymen's League four-page *Manual on Senior Citizens* (St. Louis, Missouri, re-issued Feb. 1, 1957). A packet of information for churches, *The Church's Responsibility for the Aging,* was prepared in 1960 by the Council for Christian Social Action of the United Church of Christ. Virginia Stafford's manual, *Older Adults in the Church* (The Methodist Publishing House, revised edition, 1958) is an excellent source for program planning and administration. The May, 1954, issue of *Adult Leadership* (Vol. 3, No. 1) includes an excellent symposium on a workshop that dealt with working with older people; and the September, 1954, issue of *Pastoral Psychology* (Vol. 5, No. 46) edited by Paul B.

THE CHURCH CAN HELP MEET THE SPIRITUAL NEEDS OF
OLDER PERSONS

A major function of the church is to meet the spiritual needs of people. As it meets these needs, it helps to develop individual personalities and helps to solve or to prevent many personal and social ills and problems.

It was evident from the interview excerpts in Chapters 6 and 7 and from the findings of the other studies reported on in this book that many older people have inadequate interpretations of the doctrines of their church. To whatever extent sound doctrine promotes personal adjustment, these people are lacking the full benefit of the church's potential contribution to their lives. Some of them may never have been members of study groups systematically learning Christian theology and its implications for living. Others may have been exposed only to incompetent teaching, which led them to pick up a hodgepodge of erroneous interpretations and a jumble of unintegrated ideas. If a basic task of the church is to teach spiritual lessons, there is reason to believe that it may have failed in this task for many of the older members that were studied (although the various research projects were not aimed at discovering whether that was so).

The church program of religious education needs improvement not only for persons in the later years of life but also at every earlier level, so that the doctrines brought by church members with them into old age from the younger periods of life will not have to be unlearned and replaced by corrected concepts when they become elderly. In its emphasis upon meeting the needs of people in this life on earth, the church must neither forget the part it ought to play in preparing people for life beyond the grave nor think that its sole task is to promote adjustment to temporal conditions.

Maves is devoted to articles on the church and older people. What various denominations were doing for older people was summarized in "Forsake Me Not" by Margaret Frakes, *Christian Century*, 72:1268-1270, Nov. 2, 1955, and interdenominational programs were presented in her "Fellowship in Ministering," *Christian Century*, 72:1297-1299, Nov. 9, 1955. (The last two articles are part of a series of eight that deal with the church and older people.) A highly suggestive presentation of what the church can do to help meet needs of older people is *The Fulfillment Years in Christian Education*, the report of the International Conference on the Church and Older Persons held at Williams Bay, Wisconsin, and sponsored by the Division of Christian Education, National Council of the Churches of Christ in the U.S.A., July 26-Aug. 1, 1953.

Many older people have a sense of insecurity, a feeling of insignificance, a fear of death, or a sense of regret for certain past mistakes or failures. To these the message of the Christian church brings comfort and assurance. It offers opportunities for service that can restore a feeling of importance and worth to the individual, opportunities for worship that can impart a sense of security in a world of uncertainties, opportunities for confession and forgiveness that can take away the sting of regret, and opportunities for the exercise of faith in the promise of God that He will never leave nor forsake the one who is trusting in Him. "Death education" to provide a balanced and wholesome point of view on death is one task of the church.[3]

To those who are frustrated in the failure to make sense of life as they have experienced it, the church offers a basic attitude toward life that will develop a sense of serenity and feelings of security; to those who feel unwanted, it offers the assurance of God's continuing love; to those who are lonely, it offers fellowship in the church as well as the assurance of the omnipresence of God; to those who are self-centered, it offers a perspective that includes all mankind for eternity as well as for time.[4]

There are various ways in which the church imparts these spiritual benefits to its older constituents. Not only can it use the usual channels of worship and prayer services, but it can also work through effective programs of pastoral counseling and care of the aged and infirm. The spiritual message of the church can be conveyed through tape-recorded services played back to the shut-ins during the week, perhaps under sponsorship of a young people's group or some other organization, and through special services such as "gospel team" meetings for shut-ins and for the residents of old people's homes and convalescent homes. Special classes in the church school and training program can encourage them to share in the study of the Bible and to learn the application of Scriptural principles to their own specific needs. Transportation can be provided to

3. Joseph R. Sizoo, "The Answer of Christian Faith," in Janet H. Baird (ed.), These Harvest Years, Doubleday and Co., 1951, pp. 247-263, and H. Lee Jacobs, "Spiritual Resources for the Aged in Facing the Problem of Death," Adding Life to Years, Vol. 6, No. 3, pp. 3-8, Mar., 1959.

4. Federal Security Agency, Man and His Years: An Account of the First National Conference on Aging, Health Publications Institute, 1931, pp. 206-210.

help those no longer able to attend church services without special help. Publications of the local church as well as of denominational and interdenominational bodies can contribute to the spiritual edification of older people. Serving of Communion to the shut-in at home or in the hospital and various other activities of the church and its pastor can help promote the spiritual life of its older members.

THE CHURCH CAN EDUCATE

Through its educational program the church can help eliminate common errors about old age and the aged from the minds of older people themselves as well as from the minds of younger people. It can help educate the aged so that they can become better persons, and it can help younger people prepare for old age.

Numerous mistaken notions about old age and old people can be dispelled and eliminated through the educational work of the church.[5] One of these is the idea that old people are nearly all the same — that they are *old* often makes us forget that they are *people*.[6] They have pronounced individual differences, often to the most accentuated degree, for they have had a longer time to develop differing personalities than young people. Some older people are very conservative, but others are liberal and progressive; some are physically infirm, but others are vigorous and agile; no two are alike in every way. Since each one is different from all others, wise church leaders recognize the distinct differences between them and purposively educate people to treat each one as an individual in his own right. The church can teach that each older person should be given the right to make his own decisions, except in cases of obvious and extreme senility, and each ought to be respected as a person instead of being treated as a child just like all others who are supposedly in their second childhood.

A second error the church can help eradicate from the minds of old and young alike is the idea that the aged are no longer able to grow, to learn, to adjust to new circumstances. There

5. Cf. Paul B. Maves and J. Lennart Cedarleaf, *Older People and the Church*, Abingdon-Cokesbury Press, 1949, pp. 50-58, and Wayne E. Oates, "Attitudes Toward Aging," *Home Life*, Vol. 10, No. 1, Jan., 1956, pp. 17-20.

6. See George Lawton, "Old Age, First Person Singular," in George Lawton (ed.), *New Goals for Old Age*, Columbia University Press, 1943, p. 169, and Francis Gerty, "Importance of Individualization of Treatment in the Aging Period," *Geriatrics*, 12:123-129, 1957.

are so many problems in senescence that the individual must adjust and change.   In urbanized, industrialized civilization people have become accustomed to change to a much greater extent than in rural pastoral cultures of certain other lands and of days gone by.   As a result, they are probably more adjustable in old age than they would be had they come from the other type of background.   Yet there are many even in American cities who have immigrated from rural societies where change has taken place only very slowly.   Such persons have not had the practice of adjusting that is so characteristic of the majority; therefore, there are great variations among older people in this regard.

The older person who has been learning all his life, who has been adjusting frequently to new circumstances, and who has been growing and developing mentally can continue to do so in his old age.   The notion that "you can't teach an old dog new tricks" may apply to dogs, but it definitely does not apply to people!

A third mistaken idea the church can help correct through education is the notion that old age is an unimportant period of life when the individual can no longer be active and can no longer contribute.[7]   It is this idea which prevents many older people from trying to contribute and makes many of them feel they are now on the scrapheap with nothing to live for except the anticipation of death.   The older person, especially if he is a Christian, need not reach the scrapheap.   As long as he retains consciousness, he can contribute to the needs of others.   Even if he can do so in no other way, he can "move mountains" for others through intercessory prayer.

Older people need to feel useful in order to be well-adjusted individuals.   Their creative ability can be great, and they have much to live for if life remains meaningful to them and if their interests are kept at a high level.[8]

Many older people can continue in active employment far beyond the traditional retirement age.   When he was Secretary of Labor, James P. Mitchell reported some findings of a Department of Labor study that indicate that older workers do not lack physical steadiness of body, arm, and hand; they have better

7. See Joan M. Smith, "Psychological Understanding in Casework with the Aged," *Journal of Social Casework*, 29:188-193, May, 1948.

8. For a discussion of this see Geza Revesz, "Age and Achievement," *Hibbert Journal*, 53:273-279, Apr., 1955, and Marc H. Hollender, "Role of the Psychiatrist in Homes for the Aged," *Geriatrics*, 6:243, 1951.

attendance records at work than young people; they have fewer disabling injuries; and they are more dependable and efficient.[9]

Indirectly at least, the church can help eliminate the false idea that older people are devoid of sexual interest and drive which is sometimes reflected in calling them "the third sex." The Kinsey reports and other studies of sexual behavior of human beings indicate that many married persons continue their active sexual relationships well into the later decades of life. If they are led to think that this is abnormal or that it is sinful to retain the sexual interests considered characteristic of younger adults, serious mental — and hence spiritual — problems may result.

A fifth fallacy which the church's educational program can help correct is the idea that older people wish to be relieved of responsibility. They often do wish to be relieved of *some* responsibility and to carry a lighter load than previously, but to force them to retire suddenly and completely from all responsibility is often the equivalent of forcing them prematurely into the grave. Overprotection and overindulgence makes them feel depreciated as being incapable, incompetent and inferior. Inestimable injury to self-respect and the inner sense of worthiness results from such policies, as we saw in chapter 7.

A sixth fallacy, which many mistakenly believe, is that it is old age in and of itself that constitutes a social problem. The church has an excellent opportunity to teach that old age is natural and inevitable, but the conditions that surround the aged and the attitudes of people toward them create the problems. There is a need to recognize that the problems of old age arise from the failure to understand both the true handicaps of aged people in our society and the personal assets possessed by elderly persons.[10]

A seventh fallacy the church can correct overlaps with certain of the others. It is the mistaken idea of many churchmen that it is no use to work with the aged: They are too old to change, too old to be converted, too old to contribute to the church; if one gives any of his time as a church leader to older people, the youth work will suffer and before long nothing will be left of the congregation. Such ideas are much more

9. James P. Mitchell, "What About Older Workers?" *The American Weekly*, Sept. 4, 1955, p. 2.
10. Helen Hardy Brunot, *Old Age in New York City*, Welfare Council of New York City, 1943, pp. 7-8.

widespread in church circles than most leaders in the church care to or dare to admit.

Because the aged are so often neglected by conventional churches, they may turn to cults that entice them. In their spiritual striving and seeking in old age they will, if rebuffed or ignored, turn away from the church to the sects that are so eager to receive them.

The spiritual benefits offered through the church are not intended only for youth, although all too often its programs of evangelism would seem to indicate that. There perhaps are only two periods of life when people are more open to receive the gospel than in old age. One of these is early adolescence and the other the period of child-bearing, especially during the infancy of the first child.[11]

The church can do its part to dispel the gloom that results from these and other similar mistaken ideas held by many older people as well as by youth. It can do so through its educational program in the church school and in other areas of church life; but it can also do so through the indirect influence of pastors who do not reaffirm these stereotyped ideas in their sermons and of leaders who put older people to work in the church in such a way that they are living examples refuting the false ideas.

In addition to helping "educate away" mistaken notions about old age and older people, the church can help younger people prepare for old age. It can help them develop wholesome interests and social relationships which can be perpetuated into the later years of life, and thus it can contribute indirectly to this goal. It can help mature adults prepare for the day of retirement from work so that they will not only retire *from* but will also retire *to* something. It can help develop the adjustability and adaptability which seem so intimately related to good personal adjustment at any age. It can help develop spiritual maturity that will assist the individual facing a crisis to realize and to practice dependence upon God in the faith that comes through complete consecration to

11. This is a topic on which research is needed. In groups emphasizing the need for conversion, most conversions to Christianity occur in childhood or adolescence in our culture. This may be a result of the selective process of "weeding out" persons most prone to conversion at this early age. Does the same pattern prevail elsewhere or with all types of evangelistic outreach?

Him. The traditional adult Bible class is insufficient to meet all these needs.[12]

The church also can directly help older persons through its formal program of education. It can help them realize that there is a future for them — a future in this life as well as in the life to come. This recognition will help them to gain a new sense of importance, a feeling of belonging, a sense of direction, and a share in creative activity.[13] It can help older people face the complexities of living in our modern age through its sponsorship of church libraries, special lectures, discussion groups, extension membership in the church school,[14] and like activities. Education of older people as to the reasons for changes in our society, the backgrounds of current customs and practices, the advantages and disadvantages of alternative ways of meeting practical problems, the cooperative arrangements by which older people can help one another, and various other subjects will help them cultivate the spiritual virtues that will enable them to live more wholesome lives.

There is an additional way in which the church can be a wholesome indirect but important educator — it can educate the community as a whole. It can do so by rightfully fulfilling its place as the conscience of society and by setting a wholesome example in its own dealings with and about the aging people in its midst. The church and its members can serve as "the light of the world" with regard to moral and ethical problems, indicating to men what they ought to do and what they ought not to do. One of the ten commandments is that men ought to honor their fathers and mothers. Honor and

12. Mrs. Geneva Mathiasen, "Preparation for Retirement," *Social Action*, Vol. 26, No. 5, pp. 7-15, Jan., 1960. See also Walter Mayer, "How Can the Sunday School Help You Minister to Older People?," *Leader* (David C. Cook) , Vol. 62, No. 6, p. 3, June, 1961.

13. H. Lee Jacobs in *Iowa Conference on Gerontology*, State University of Iowa Extension Bulletin No. 703, 1955, p. 9.

14. See Mrs. Will S. McCraw, "Grandmother Joins the Sunday School," *Home Life*, Vol. 9, No. 11, Nov., 1955, p. 4. Most churches fall far short of their potential in the religious education of older people. Cf. Paul B. Maves, *The Christian Religious Education of Older People*, Department of Pastoral Services, Federal Council of the Churches of Christ in America, 1950; H. Lee Jacobs, "Old People Are Members, Too," *International Journal of Religious Education*, Vol. 35, No. 7, pp. 12-13, Mar., 1959; Virginia Stafford, "Role of the Church in Education [for the Aged and Aging]," *Adult Leadership*, Vol. 9, No. 1, pp. 16, 33, May 1960; and Rev. Walter Mayer, "How Can the Sunday School Help You Minister to Older People?" *Leader* (David C. Cook) , Vol. 62, No. 6, p. 3, June 1961.

respect for members of the older generation, according to most Hebrew and Christian interpretations, is not something intended to be limited to children only through the period of adolescence.

The church teaches by its example as much as, if not more than, by its pronouncements. If its demand for youthful pastors continues to cause premature retirement of the clergy,[15] if its lack of adequate pension plans for its employees causes them to suffer economic need in old age, if its insistence upon compulsory retirement at a fixed age forces many physically and mentally capable persons to be laid on the shelf, if its over-emphasis upon youth operates to the detriment of mature older adults in the church and in the community, then it is not only implying to the world that such practices are ethically and spiritually proper, but it is also encouraging the world to follow in its steps.[16]

If materialistic standards prevail in the church to such an extent that property, money, prestige and power are placed before the welfare of people, can it expect the rest of society to be any different? The church teaches by what it does as much as, or more than, by what it says.

THE CHURCH CAN HELP DEVELOP INDIVIDUAL PERSONALITIES

It contributes to the kind of personality adjustment and development that enables one to live through the later years of life in calm composure and true enjoyment in many ways. Potential contributions by the church to this goal can be made in the following ways, some of which will be dealt with in other contexts more fully:[17]

It can help modify the values of the society so that older people are respected as individual persons with distinct personalities. As a result, older persons will have increased self-respect.

The church can impart such spiritual benefits to its constituents that an inner security will be developed in the face

---

15. See John Irving Daniel, "Premium on Youth," *Christian Century*, 65:478-480, May 19, 1948.

16. For additional suggestions of a related nature see Federal Security Agency, *op. cit.*, pp. 218-222. Cf. S. Waldman, "Coverage of Ministers under Old-Age, Survivors and Disability Insurance," *Social Security Bulletin*, Vol. 24, No. 4, pp. 18-22, April, 1961.

17. Cf. Paul B. Maves and J. Lennart Cedarleaf, *op. cit.*, pp. 75-80.

of come-what-may. They then will have increased self-confidence — or rather God-confidence! — and will be able to face their problems more realistically and more calmly.

The church can help develop social relationships that in turn can assist the individual in the cultivation of his personality traits until he becomes a more gracious person, poised in any social situation.

The Christian church can impart to the individual goals and values for which he can live in order to receive the truly abundant life that Jesus Christ said He came to give (John 10:10). By emphasizing the importance of the individual as created in the image of God and as a soul for whom God gave His only Son, it can impart to the individual a sense of his importance and worth. This will contribute to his personality development and to good personal adjustment, if done in a way which at the same time imparts a deep sense of humility.

THE CHURCH CAN HELP MEET PHYSICAL AND MATERIAL NEEDS OF OLDER PERSONS

Groups within the church can put the teachings of the church to "bear one another's burdens" into practice by helping the aged with the literal burdens they so often are forced to carry. At moving time, the older person often is in need of help that may not be forthcoming from relatives and close friends if they are living far away or if they are engrossed in other responsibilities.

Older people often need help with heavy work around the home — the laundry, lawn-mowing, putting up storm windows, shoveling snow, etc. Some of them need assistance with their cooking and other daily needs that can best be met through regular, dependable visitors, through foster care residence with some younger family, or perhaps through moving into an old people's home.[18]

When the church cannot meet the material needs of older persons directly, it can help them find social welfare agencies

18. Visiting homemakers' services, "meals on wheels," and visiting nurse activities can be provided by churches when not otherwise available in a community. See Mark P. Hale, "Foster Home Care for the Aged," *Geriatrics*, 13:116-119, 1958. Research demonstrates that twice as many aged Americans would pefer to get help from the church rather than from the government if special care outside the family becomes necessary. (James W. Wiggins and Helmut Schoeck, "A Profile of the Aging: U.S.A.," *Geriatrics*, 16:336-342, July 1961.)

and personnel which can help meet those needs. When the pastor or some other representative of the church realizes that serious physical or mental ailments may be present, he can encourage and help the older person to visit the medical doctor or psychiatrist who may be of assistance or to find other appropriate and competent help.

In some churches employment agencies with lay leadership can help able persons who are in their later maturity find part-time or full-time work. Even unpaid positions in the church itself often are left unfilled when organized efforts could produce capable volunteers from its own membership.

Churches have often established old people's homes and will no doubt continue to do so in the future. These homes, however, should be looked upon as a place in which to live rather than as merely a place to die.[19] They should be so named that people will not think of them in the same category as mental institutions or county poor farms. Needless to say, the standards and staffs of these church-sponsored homes should be of the highest quality.[20]

THE CHURCH CAN HELP MEET THE SOCIAL AND RECREATIONAL NEEDS OF OLDER PEOPLE

One of the needs of mankind is for social fellowship and group participation. This need, for many people at least, is not satisfied in the family and other informal groups of which they are a part. Many churches can organize groups specifically for older people, not to function only in the Sunday school

19. Ralph E. Shannon in *Iowa Conference on Gerontology, op. cit.,* pp. 8f.

20. See suggestions in Federal Security Agency, *op. cit.,* pp. 215-218. For an excellent presentation of wholesome activity programs in homes for the aged, see Catherine Lee Wahlstrom, *Add Life to Their Years,* National Council of the Churches of Christ in the U.S.A., 1953. A discussion of current trends in the administration of church-sponsored homes for the aged may be found in Margaret Frakes, "A Desired Haven," *Christian Century,* 72:1397-1399, Nov. 30, 1955, and "If Ye Have Not Love," *ibid.,* 72:1426-1429, Dec. 7, 1955. Thorough outlines of goals, facilities, services, and administration of homes for the aged are presented in *A Guide for Lutheran Homes Serving the Aged,* Division of Welfare, National Lutheran Council, 1957, and *Sheltered Care for Older Persons,* The Methodist Church Board of Hospitals and Homes, 1955. See also Daniel J. Hafrey, "Presbyterian Village," *Geriatrics,* 14:728-733, Nov., 1959, and, for a description of an excellent program, Mother M. Bernadette de Lourdes, *et al., Where Somebody Cares,* G. P. Putnam's Sons, 1960.

but also during the long days of the week between Sundays.[21] Other churches can counsel and refer older persons to community organizations that can meet many of these needs.

Golden Age clubs and similar organizations, even when not sponsored directly by the church, often use church facilities and function with the assistance of church personnel.

Theological seminaries have the opportunity to meet the increasing demand for well-balanced recreational programs for older parishioners by placing their students in homes for the aged for training. Volunteers for the leadership of programs of these kinds can come from the church.[22] The theological orientation of a church will, of course, decide the nature and scope of its services to the leisure-time needs of older people.

Ideally, recreational programs sponsored for older people should be in the hands of the older persons themselves to as great an extent as is possible. Members of the church fellowship or of auxiliaries to the church can find opportunities for service to their own age group as well as to others through the church, as will be emphasized in the next chapter. They can cultivate a sense of fellowship with one another as they engage in various corporate activities, such as worship. As they develop new friendships and new responsibilities, their needs for personal recognition will be satisfied. They will enjoy pleasant relaxation in social groups. Their minds will be kept alert as they keep up-to-date on what is occurring in the world and as they gain new ideas to think about.

As much as possible older people should be integrated into existing groups, and services for them should be a normal part of the entire life of the church.[23] It is often difficult to enroll them in new groups that are identified — rightly or wrongly — as groups just for old people, for many are reluctant

21. See, e.g., William Kincaid Newman, "Our Senior Citizens," *Church Management,* Vol. 36, No. 8, pp. 16, 18, 20, May 1960.

22. Jerome Kaplan, *A Social Program for Older People,* University of Minnesota Press, 1953, p. 28. See also Robert J. Havighurst and Ruth Albrecht, *op. cit.,* pp. 205-207.

23. Oscar P. Campbell, "Organizing Older Adults in the Church," *International Journal of Religious Education,* Vol. 30, No. 2, Oct., 1953, pp. 6f.; Charles W. Garrett, *A Curriculum Structure for Older Persons in the Church Based upon a Study of the Opinions of Ministers and Older Persons,* Ph.D. thesis, New York University, 1953, p. 186; and William T. Swaim, Jr., *The Church's Ministry to Older Adults,* The Presbyterian Homes of Central Pennsylvania, 1953, p. 1.

to admit that they are old. They feel they will always be "young at heart" or "young in spirit," so why should they be singled out for membership in an old folks' group? Being a part of the church fellowship will contribute far more to their happiness than being kept apart from it.

Some good advice to the church that plans to organize group activities for older people in the local church came from a group that met under the leadership of Catherine Wahlstrom at the International Conference on the Church and Older Persons in 1953. They suggested that the interests, hobbies and backgrounds of group members should be known; the group should elect its own officers and plan its own programs; the program should be kept flexible and should change as the interests of the group change; community resources should be used; the program should be person-centered, not activity-centered; interests should be discovered through such devices as checklists and observation; leaders should not be over-protective of older adults in program activities; responsibility should be delegated so as to be shared by all, and a patient and democratic attitude should be manifest instead of one that emphasizes speed, which can result only from autocratic leadership.[24]

In various ways even older persons who are homebound can be helped to retain a sense of belonging to the groups in which they formerly were active: as members visit them, as a visitation committee does its work, as they are supplied with the study and worship materials used by the group, as they are given

24. Viola K. Braun, "Older Adults Need Fellowship," *International Journal of Religious Education*, Vol. 30, No. 3, Nov., 1953, p. 22. Illustrations of what is being done in Protestant, Jewish, and Catholic churches, especially in groups organized or conducted for educational purposes, may be found in Wilma T. Donahue (compiler), *Education for Later Maturity: A Handbook*, Whiteside and William Morrow and Co., 1955, pp. 198-222. Excellent suggestions for recreational programs and activities may be found in *Recreation for the Aging* prepared by Arthur Williams for the National Recreation Association, Association Press, 1953; Chapter 12 deals specifically with the church. *Group Work With the Aged* by Susan H. Kubie and Gertrude Landau, International Universities Press, 1953, is a record of nine years of work in a recreation center for the aged; it can yield valuable suggestions to any discerning group leader of older people. A folio of suggestions and aids, "Planning a Club Program for Older People," has been prepared by Rev. A. Rismiller, Geriatrics Chaplain, The Lutheran Welfare League of Central Ohio, 102 S. Gift St., Columbus, Ohio.

greetings on special occasions, as they are given special programs on occasional visits of groups from the church.[25]

In his well-known book, *Man, the Unknown,* Alexis Carrel has said that for the old leisure is even more dangerous than for the young. The time of the aging individual should be "filled with mental and spiritual adventures" to enrich his declining years.[26] The church can do much to meet this need of its older constituents.

THE CHURCH CAN HELP OLDER PEOPLE SOLVE THEIR PERSONAL PROBLEMS

Many personal problems often confront the older person that are entirely new to him. He is expected to manage an estate of a deceased brother or sister, to arrange for the collection of insurance or a pension, to dispose of real estate that has been in the family all his lifetime, to make a will, or to take care of other personal and legal affairs for which he may be ill-equipped or not equipped at all by past experience or training. The well-trained pastor can do much to help with many of the personal problems that confront the older person in the church, and he can lead the older person to the lawyer, social worker, or other professional person in the community who is best qualified to help solve his specific problems.

Pastoral counseling of older people often deals with problems that do not at first glance seem to be spiritual at all — problems such as those mentioned in the preceding paragraph, problems of money, problems of social relationships, problems associated with adjustment to retirement, etc. The wise pastor will profit from the experiences of others through wide reading about the problems and techniques of counseling, through discussions with other clergymen to share one another's insights, and, if at all possible, through special training in formal educational settings even after graduation from theological seminary.[27] He will then be able to help alleviate the problems and fears of older people.

25. Oscar P. Campbell, *op. cit.,* p. 7.
26. Alexis Carrel, *Man, the Unknown,* Harper & Brothers, 1939, p. 186.
27. Many excellent suggestions are found in Paul B. Maves and J. Lennart Cedarleaf, *op. cit.,* especially in Chapter VI, "Principles and Methods of Pastoral Care," pp. 108-135. See also Harlow Donovan, "Pastoral Needs of Older Women," *Journal of Pastoral Care,* 10:170-176, Fall, 1956; Marian Emery, "Casework with the Aging — Today's Frontier," *Social Casework,* 39:455-458, October, 1958; and the symposium, "Casework with the Aging," *Social Casework,* 42:219-290, May-June 1961.

The church can help to solve and to prevent many personal problems of older people by encouraging them to retire *to* something rather than simply to retire *from* their work and the world. It can encourage them to develop old hobbies and leisure-time interests and to find new ones, to learn what they have long desired to know, to do what they like to do, to make new friends while not neglecting the old, to live in and for the present as much or more than in and for the past, and to forget themselves in loving service to others who are in need.

Older persons who are in fellowship with one another through the social activities of the church or its auxiliary groups also have the opportunity to get help from others in their group whom they respect and whom they can trust. As older persons help one another, they give to one another many of the satisfactions of recognition and responsibility that most people desire.

The church can also assist in promoting the personal adjustment of older people by deliberately finding a place of usefulness for each one. As the personal abilities and interests of the older person are recognized, the sense of personal worth is fostered. When he is given important tasks to perform which he recognizes to be truly important and not simply make-work or keep-busy projects, he will become a happier person.

THE CHURCH CAN ADAPT ITS PHYSICAL FACILITIES TO THE NEEDS AND PROBLEMS OF OLDER PEOPLE

To many this has meant only such limited services as the placing of special hearing aids in the pews for the hard-of-hearing. Actually, facilities of this kind are often unused in the churches that have them because they are located in such a position that the person using them feels he is singled out and made conspicuous by their use.

More important, however, are the location of rest rooms where they can be reached conveniently by the aged and infirm, the avoidance of long flights of steps, non-glare lighting, skid-proof wax on floors, radiant heating, pews from which it is easy to arise, convenient location with respect to transportation facilities, and similar considerations.[28]

28. F. Grover Fulkerson, "Older Adults in the Church Building," *International Journal of Religious Education*, Vol. 30, No. 11, July-Aug., 1954, pp. 12-14.

THE CHURCH CAN COOPERATE IN RESEARCH STUDIES

Social and behavioral scientists are increasingly turning their attention toward the field of gerontology, the study of aging. Often through the church it is possible to gather information that can be used to test hypotheses and develop theories about the aged and their problems and about the solutions to these problems. The church can help researchers to gain access to older persons who would not be readily available to them otherwise and to secure cooperation from suspicious older people who would, without church help, be reluctant to give the confidential information that is sometimes needed for scientific studies.

Some churches may even be called upon to set up experimental educational or social programs which can be observed carefully by researchers over a period of time to determine their effects. As they cooperate with one another, scientists and churchmen alike will benefit, but the greatest benefit of all will come to older people themselves.

THE CHURCH CAN USE ITS INFLUENCE IN CIVIC AND POLITICAL AFFAIRS

When there is a need for a special community center for older people, for social and recreational organizations on the behalf of older persons in the community, or for other civic projects for human welfare, the church can encourage citizens under its influence to stand for that position which is consistent with Christian principles of justice, kindness and love.

Similarly, the church can encourage the passage and administration of federal, state and local laws which directly or indirectly promote the financial security, the independence, and the general welfare of older people. In so doing, the church will indirectly contribute to the enhancement of the personal dignity of every person in the nation.

THE CHURCH CAN STUDY ITS COMMUNITY

Churches can help make community surveys which include analysis of the number, characteristics, and needs of the aged, existing programs for them, program objectives and effectiveness, leadership, and general evaluation. Such studies can contribute to mutual improvement of church-related and non-church activities for older people. As a result of these surveys, the church will often be led to introduce programs and

activities for the aged into its own work at the same time as
it leads in community action on their behalf.[29]

CONCLUSION

It may seem to the reader to whom this field of knowledge
is new that the ten suggestions and their numerous subsidiary
implications which are given in this chapter are visionary,
impractical, ivory-tower speculations. In fact, however, every
one of these is being practiced in some place or other.

In 1954 a systematic survey was made of fifty-four churches
in Greater Winnipeg, Canada, to obtain information of their
interests and activities in relation to older people. Twenty-
eight (fifty-two per cent) of these churches reported that they
fitted the elderly members of their congregation into the general scheme of observances and activities and did not have
special clubs or services for them. Twenty-three said they
had made referrals to hospitals and other health agencies; nineteen reported organized plans for visiting the sick and infirm;
twenty-one had referred older members to welfare agencies for
specific kinds of help; three gave weekly and two gave monthly
lunches for aged persons; three sponsored clubs for older people
of both sexes; two sponsored separate clubs for aged men and
for aged women. One church sponsored two housing projects,
one of which was for couples and the other for single persons,
and in addition it served a free meal once a week during the
winter months for aged persons.[30] The churches of large cities
in the United States often provide similar activities and services for older persons.

Older persons themselves desire services from their churches
of the kinds suggested in this chapter. A representative cross-
section of older people in Long Beach, California, gives a direct indication of the wishes of senior citizens aged sixty-five
years and over in that city. Of the 606 persons in the sample,
one out of five (120) believed that the churches were not taking sufficient interest in older people. Over half of these gave
definite suggestions of things the churches ought to do for older
people. The major suggestions they made, in declining order
of frequency mentioned, were that the church should make

29. For instance, a survey of parishes in the Episcopal Diocese of Dallas
discovered numerous unrecognized and unmet needs pertinent to the aged
and aging. ("Summary of Survey on Needs of Aging Persons in Parishes
and Missions," E. D. Farmer Foundation, Dallas, 1960, Mimeographed.)

30. Committee on Services for the Aged, *Age and Opportunity*, Welfare
Council of Greater Winnipeg, 1956, p. 39.

home visits, organize special groups for social purposes, provide transportation to church, employ church workers experienced in working with senior citizens, and organize special groups for worship.[31]

In the Long Beach study, it was found that over half (fifty-two per cent) of the 606 interviewees reported their church attendance to be less frequent than it had been ten years previously, while 35.3 per cent indicated they were attending "about the same" and 11.5 per cent reported their church attendance to be "more often." The reasons given for attending church less often than previously lend additional support to the validity of many of the suggestions in this chapter. In declining order of frequency suggested, the tabulated reasons are health or physical condition, listening to services on radio and television, loss of interest, transportation difficulties, lack of acquaintance with the people now in church, and "cannot afford to go to church."[32]

These suggestions are already in effect in many places, and they are desired by many older people. Some are a natural outgrowth of the work of the church even when no special consideration is given to the aged as such, and others are a part of explicit, deliberately planned programs designed to meet the specific needs of the aged. Few churches have the personnel and other resources to put all of these suggestions into immediate practice, but all can introduce some of them as integral parts of their total program of worship and service to God and man.[33] To do so is not costly[34] except in terms of sacrificial love and consecrated time on the part of church leaders and workers. In fact, in terms of humanitarian and spiritual values, *not* to do so is tremendously expensive.

31. Charles W. McCann, *Long Beach Senior Citizens Survey*, Long Beach Community Welfare Council, 1955, p. 53.

32. *Ibid.*, p. 52.

33. Additional descriptions of church programs are given in George Gleason, *Horizons for Older People*, The Macmillan Co., 1956; Sidney Entman, "The Ministry of Organized Religion to the Jewish Aged — Its Philosophy and Practice," in Delton L. Scudder, editor, *Organized Religion and the Older Person*, University of Florida Press, 1958, pp. 34-42; Gordon Poteat, "The Ministry of Organized Religion to the Aged," in *ibid.*, pp. 43-52; Newman M. Biller, "The Role of the Synagogue in Work with Old People," *Jewish Social Service Quarterly*, 28:284-289, Mar., 1952, and "Super Sixty Clubs," Department of Social Relations, The (Episcopal) Diocese of Washington, D. C., n.d.

34. Ed., "Church Services to Elderly Need Not Be Costly," *Christian Century*, 76:1428-1429, Dec. 9, 1959.

CHAPTER 9

WHAT OLDER PERSONS CAN DO FOR THE CHURCH

POPULAR PRESENTATIONS OFTEN IMPLY that the sole end of life is to live a comfortable old age. This philosophy can lead to abject dependence and absurd selfishness.[1] Older people wish to feel useful, to continue contributing actively to the welfare of others, to feel wanted because of their contributions. One of the major outlets for their abilities can be the church and its auxiliary organizations and activities.

The suggestions in this chapter indicate some of the outlets of service that are available or can be made available to older members of the local church. Not all of them will apply to every older person because of the differences in personalities and abilities found among them, but every older person will find several places he can fill in the work of the church.

OLDER PERSONS CAN PARTICIPATE IN THE WORSHIP SERVICES OF THE CHURCH

They can actively as well as passively participate when they are called upon to lead in public prayer, to give a testimony to the assembled fellowship of how the Lord has led them through life or through certain trials or to speak in other ways.

Sometimes older people, when given opportunity for public testimony, do not seem to know when they ought to stop speaking. Wise leadership can help solve that problem, but it can also be solved in part by giving them more regular and more frequent opportunities to speak. If they are called upon only rarely, they may feel that they must express all that is on their minds. If more opportunities are given to speak in their own groups and in such other situations as the Sunday evening or midweek service of the church, they will usually say less on any one given occasion.

1. See John R. Voris, "Let Senior Citizens Serve Others!," *Christian Century*, 77:251-252, Mar. 2, 1960.

Through both active and passive participation in the services of the church, the older person as well as the younger one develops a sense of fellowship and of belonging that is important to his personal adjustment and hence to the spiritual as well as the social well-being of his life.

OLDER PEOPLE CAN ENGAGE IN THEIR OWN PERSONAL DEVOTIONAL ACTIVITIES

This may appear to be a purely personal matter, but it can be a source of spiritual strength that indirectly will be imparted to others and as such becomes a type of service to the church.

Reading the Bible and meditating upon its contents can be a major source of peace and comfort. The use of devotional literature prepared by the church, such as the monthly and quarterly booklets of daily meditations, Bible readings, and prayers prepared by various denominations, can be of great assistance to the person who wishes to see the practical implications and applications of the Book of books.[2]

The answers to perplexing problems will be found, in many instances, as the older person searches the Scriptures in the faith that they contain God's message to him.

Many are assisted in their religious devotional activities by various symbolic objects (works of art, pictures, candles, etc.) or by having a specific place of worship in the home, a "prayer closet," or a "family altar." Even though God does not dwell in temples made by hands, these tangible objects help many older people who have dulled senses of communication cultivate a sense of the presence of God and of His watchcare over them, as well as a heightened sense of the fellowship of believers. These are then, subconsciously if not consciously, communicated to others who associate with them.

Many are the pastors and laymen who have visited ill and infirm "saints of God" who were in great pain and suffering only to come away with far greater encouragement and help to their own souls than they felt they had imparted to the shut-in person.

2. Available devotional literature published for the use of older people includes Paul B. Maves, *The Best Is Yet to Be,* Westminster Press, 1951; Charles A. Behnke, *New Frontiers for Spiritual Living,* Concordia Publishing House, 1959, and Glenn H. Asquith, *Lively May I Walk,* Abingdon Press, 1960.

Older persons can pray

Not only can they pray for themselves and their own needs, as is implied in the preceding section, but they can also intercede with God on behalf of others. Even the bedridden older person who may never be able to leave his bed until death can through prayer develop a sense of participation in interpersonal relationships with God and with the innumerable host of fellow believers of the past, present and future. The Christian confined to the sickroom or bound by infirmities to his home can still be a co-worker with God and with his fellowmen as he engages in intercessory prayer.

The older Christian who lives in intimate fellowship with his Lord is never laid on the shelf. As long as he retains consciousness in this life and is not in such extreme suffering that all thoughts except those of his pain are squeezed from his mind, he can be active in the service of God, the church and his fellowmen through his prayers on their behalf.

Older persons can teach others in the church

Many older people can serve God and the church by teaching adult or sometimes even children's classes in the church school.[3] Some of them can sponsor scout groups and teach craft classes. Many of them are also able to teach indirectly by indicating some of the experiences of the church in the past when experimental programs have been introduced. Their knowledge and skills often can be a valuable source of insight into the practical problems of the church and a valuable source of service graciously donated to the church "as unto the Lord."

Older persons can help in the visitation program of the church

Many older adults can be used in some form of visitation for the church.[4] Some can welcome and register guests when they arrive in the church school or at the worship services; some can visit the sick; some can visit newcomers to the community to invite them to the church; some can visit prospective members; some can help cultivate a sense of fellowship in the church by visiting with church members. Reports to the pas-

3. Harold H. Hazenfield, "Older Adults Can Serve the Church," *International Journal of Religious Education*, Vol. 30, No. 5, Jan., 1954, pp. 16-17.
4. *Ibid.*

tor on their visits can be of great help to him by relieving him of the responsibility of visiting many guests who are members of another church in the community and visited simply out of curiosity; of visiting some of the sick; and of some other responsibilities that otherwise he might feel pressing upon him to hinder other phases of his ministry.

Various studies have established the fact that the fellowship within the church and the efforts of lay members to build up the membership are more effective than at least the initial visits of the pastor.[5] Older members can play a major part in the missionary outreach — the evangelistic emphasis — of the local church. Their testimony of the satisfactions achieved through their religion and the church can be a major influence attracting others into the church fellowship.

OLDER PERSONS CAN HELP IMPROVE AND MAINTAIN CHURCH PROPERTY[6]

Many churches are poorly landscaped and have grounds that are poorly tended. The lawn often looks unkempt alongside those of residences in the vicinity. Flowers are not cultivated properly. Shrubbery is often not trimmed when and as it ought to be. Many older people, feeling incapable of teaching or of visiting on behalf of the church, can be made to realize that gardening and lawn-tending on the church premises can be a significant service.

Many churches need remodeling, painting, storage cabinets or even additional class rooms. Many older people, retired from their regular occupation, have abilities that can be used to meet these needs in the church. They may be used either as volunteers or as paid part-time workers.

In the average church there are nearly always minor repairs needed on squeaky chairs used in the church school, bulletin boards that are marred so badly as to be unsightly, coat racks that have been broken or loosened, upholstered chairs that have become dirty or badly worn, broken toys in the nursery, etc. Here, too, the time and the talents or hobbies of many older people can be used to good advantage for the repair of these church properties.

5. One of these is by Roy G. Francis, Charles E. Ramsey, and Jacob A. Toews, "The Church in the Rural Fringe," *Minnesota Farm and Home Science,* Vol. 12, No. 2, Feb., 1955, pp. 8, 13.
6. Many of these suggestions come from Harold H. Hazenfield, *op. cit.*

Sunday school teachers are often young adults with the pressures of growing children and other duties upon them. Older people can often help them prepare materials used in the class activities.

In some churches older people serve as custodians of the church property. If the right person is secured, he will consider such work to be a special service to God and not merely a job to be done. When that is true, a pride and interest will be taken in the task that will make the church much more attractive, usable and effective in its work than might otherwise be the case.

OLDER PERSONS CAN HELP WITH THE CLERICAL WORK OF THE CHURCH

Older people who have clerical, teaching, or other white-collar or professional experience often can use their abilities in the writing and editing of a church paper or of the church bulletin, in the keeping of detailed church-school records that can improve the follow-up work of the staff, in the addressing and mailing of church announcements, in the compilation of missionary and other scrapbooks that can be used by teachers in the church-school and by leaders of auxiliary organizations of the church, in the building of historical archives which record the establishment and growth of the church and the community, in the maintenance of a church library, in the conducting of surveys or other research, and in similar activities.

Many of these avenues of service by older people can save long hours of work for the pastor, both by making it unnecessary for him or his secretary to do some of the work and by saving time in finding desired material at the time of writing a history for a church anniversary, writing the obituary of a long-time member, or seeking an incident for a sermon or sermon illustration from the archives of the church.

OLDER PERSONS CAN HELP CONDUCT THE BUSINESS OF THE CHURCH

Churches often are engaged in buying and sometimes in disposing of property. Many of them are occupied with building programs that take hours of work by the pastor or by others in the church. If competent retired people are members in the church, they can relieve the clergy and other personnel of much of the tedious detail work that takes energy away from their other duties.

Older people can serve as members of a "Volunteer Christian Corps," as Professor Elton Trueblood suggests, after their retirement from secular occupations. Some of them can serve even as business managers for the church.[7]

Both as the official representatives of the church and as its constituents in the community they can help make its outreach into and its influence upon civic affairs and community organizations more effective.

OLDER PERSONS CAN PARTICIPATE IN ORGANIZED GROUPS FOR OLDER PEOPLE

This may seem to be a purely selfish and self-centered activity, but in helping to establish and support such groups the older person helps others as well as himself. He is given an increased sense of usefulness as he helps others find that same sense of worth. He eases his own loneliness as he helps alleviate the loneliness of others. He finds work for himself as he seeks jobs for other senior adults. He makes new friends as he helps others develop friendships. He finds pleasure and joy as he tries to make others happy. His own personal problems are mitigated as he helps others find solutions or help for their difficulties. His own burdens are lifted in the process of helping to lift the burdens of his fellowmen.

OLDER PERSONS CAN HELP WITH NUMEROUS "MINOR" TASKS IN THE CHURCH[8]

They can be assigned to help usher, regulate the temperature of the church, decorate the church with flowers appropriately placed and arranged, direct traffic in the church parking lot,

7. Elton Trueblood, *Your Other Vocation*, Harper and Brothers, 1952, pp. 53f. For one account of a person who did this, see "Pastor's Right-Hand Man," *Christian Life*, Vol. 17, No. 8, Dec., 1955, pp. 51f. In some denominations older adults are permitted to become clergymen after a period of preparation. The most systematic program assisting in such a change of vocation is in the Episcopal Church. See Hartzell Spence, "Parsons-Come-Lately," *Saturday Evening Post*, Vol. 232, No. 9, pp. 13ff., Aug. 29, 1959.

8. See Marion P. Obenhaus, "Lights Under a Bushel," *International Journal of Religious Education*, Vol. 30, No. 10, June, 1954, pp. 6f., for many suggestions, and David O. Byler, "Utilizing Older Adults in the Music Ministry," *The Church Musician*, Vol. 10, No. 7, July, 1959, pp. 11-12, 14.

prepare and serve food for the church's social gatherings, guide young people in the selection of vocations, serve in the church's music ministry, speak to various groups in the church about the customs of days gone by, and represent the church in civic organizations in the community. In these and numerous other ways they can provide the seemingly small services which are seldom noticed when they are performed well but are usually obvious when they are left undone.

CONCLUSION

As the services of older people are used in the church — and they will not be used unless there is wise leadership that invites and encourages them to be of service — the church will benefit and the older persons themselves will prosper.

Intelligent study of the needs of the church and of the interests and abilities of its senior members can lead to a matching of these needs and abilities. As a result, both the church and its older members will benefit, the roles of both the young and the old in the church will be modified, and the entire program of the church will take on renewed vigor and gain increased respect in the community. The influence and service of the church can be greatly extended with almost no monetary cost through voluntary lay workers. In the year 1958, for example, forty-five lay men and women donated 15,620 hours to the Senior Citizen Project of the San Francisco Council of Churches.[9]

In the early Christian church the apostles had the church select seven men to relieve them of the task of "serving tables" and taking care of the daily distribution of material goods so that they could spend more time in prayer, the ministry of the word and preaching (Acts 6:1-6). Similarly today it is appropriate for Christian clergymen to use laymen to the fullest advantage for the routine duties of the church so that the clergy can engage in their ministry of teaching, preaching, praying, studying and counseling. It is only logical that able older persons who have much time on their hands should be used extensively in this type of service.

As the older person loses his life in sincere service to his

9. Mrs. Milton Schiffman, "Report for 1958, Senior Citizen Project, San Francisco Council of Churches," *Maturity*, Vol. 6, No. 1, pp. 15-16, Mar. 31, 1959. The minimum monetary equivalent of this donated time was $39,050.

God, his church and his fellowmen, available evidence indicates that he is more likely to find the "abundant life," the life that is characterized by good personal and social adjustment. It is indeed more blessed, more conducive to happiness in old age, to give than it is to receive.

Old age can be "the last of life for which the first was planned," a time of happiness and contentment, or it can be the most miserable period of life. It is he who gives the most in old age who in turn receives the most. This giving can continue even by the shut-in person who may not leave his home until his body is prepared for the grave, just as it can by the older person who is physically and mentally in the best of health.

Both the teachings of America's religions and the implicit values of her social scientists include the goal of making old age a time of satisfaction and joy, of good personal and social adjustment rather than of mental anguish and social maladjustment. Many programs of churches and findings of scientific studies, such as those reported in this book, are contributing to the attainment of that goal.[10]

10. Numerous studies and reports from the fifty states included in the 7,970-page *Background Studies Prepared by State Committees for the White House Conference on Aging* (86th Congress, 2d Session, Committee Print, U.S. Government Printing Office, 14 volumes, 1960) substantiate our conclusions, support our recommendations, and demonstrate the practicality of our suggestions.

APPENDIX I

THE 1961 WHITE HOUSE CONFERENCE ON AGING BASIC POLICY STATEMENTS AND RECOMMENDATIONS OF THE SECTION ON RELIGION*

THE MEANING OF LIFE is to be found solely in man's relationship to God. It is this relationship which gives meaning to all human values. In the light of it, every period of life, including that of old age, is possessed of intrinsic value and sublime potential. Viewed in the light of an eternal destiny, old age is seen to have an importance as great as that of youth or the middle years. To young and old, the divine imperative is addressed: "Thou shalt love the Lord thy God . . . and thy neighbor as thyself."

ROLE OF RELIGION IN THE LIFE OF THE OLDER PERSON

Religion's concern with human dignity at every stage in the span of life derives from the fact that each individual is created in the image of God. As a consequence, religion seeks to build a living fellowship of believers in which the aging find and share the true benefits of being a part of the household of God. It is this conviction which likewise demands a concern for such matters as the maintenance of social welfare institutions by religious bodies and the proper conduct of those sponsored by Government or voluntary agencies in a manner consonant with the nature of man and the sanctity of existence. Similarly, it is the basis of a concern for the right of every individual to a burial befitting human dignity.

It has been suggested that "man's potential for change and growth is much greater than we are willing to admit and that old age be regarded not as the age of stagnation but as the age of opportunities for inner growth." In light of this, congregations should recognize that their elder members are often specially endowed with gifts of wisdom, serenity and understanding. To the aging person, religion extends an invitation to see the later years of his life as "rich in possibilities to unlearn the follies of a lifetime, to see through inbred

* The 1961 White House Conference on Aging: Basic Policy Statements and Recommendations, 87th Congress, 1st Session, Committee Print, Prepared for the Special Committee on Aging, United States Senate, U.S. Government Printing Office, 1961, pp. 122-125.

self-deceptions, to deepen understanding and compassion, to widen the horizon of honesty, to refine the sense of fairness." The religious community assists the older person to deepen his relationship to God and to accept the assurance of eternal life.

Recommendations

So that religion may play its full and proper part in the life of the aging, it is recommended that care be exercised to provide suitable transportation and facilities for participation in worship and services with congregations. In order to reach the shut-ins, greater use should be made of religious radio, TV, and recordings, as well as the personal ministries of members and leaders. It is urged, also, that State, county and municipal governments recognize the need for more chaplaincy services in public institutions caring for the aging. Ways of providing such services should be studied on local, State and national levels by religious bodies and public agencies.

The role of the older person in the congregation

Within the life of the congregation each older person should be treated as an individual. Each is entitled to responsible membership within the religious fellowship. Any attitude on the part of the congregation which hinders the exercise of this right must be regarded as a contradiction of religious teaching. It should rather be its concern to foster relationships calculated to imbue in the elderly a sense of belonging, of being needed and useful in a vital way. This will go far to promote a richer religious experience for the aging and will likewise provide a salutary example to be followed in the family circle and in the outer rings of society.

Specifically, responsible membership should involve all or some of the following roles: That of worshipper, learner, teacher, counselor, leader or elder, volunteer aide, and member in congregational organizations. When congregations overemphasize some of these roles and under-emphasize others, older persons often are placed at a disadvantage. We affirm that these roles are all significant.

It is recommended that the congregation study the age and sex composition of its membership with a view to determining whether the prevailing distribution of roles and the available congregational organizations allow adequate outlet for the abilities, experience and needs of older members.

Role of the congregation in affecting attitudes toward older people

We underline the obligation of religious groups to instill, as an essential of sound family life, an attitude of respect for the individuality and intrinsic importance of each aging member. Thus, while both the family and the congregation will feel direct responsibility to provide special services, educational materials, and programs for the aging, every effort should be made to see that these do not involve an unnecessary separation from the main stream of familial or congregational life. It is urged, also, that all congregations make their services available to non-members.

RECOMMENDATIONS

Our society, by reason of its preoccupation with frontier development and economic advance, has tended to glorify youth and denigrate old age. The time has come to recognize that the "cult of eternal youth is idolatry." The congregations must reaffirm by teaching, by the example of their own practice and by preparation for the aging, the religious conviction of the beauty and worth of old age. We further urge that religious bodies make a greater use of radio, TV, drama, and other media in affecting changes of attitudes toward older persons.

To the end that our congregations may better instill proper attitudes toward the aging, greater provision should be made for specialized training of the clergy and of lay workers in understanding and serving the needs and potentialities of old age. This means workshops, seminars and refresher programs for those in active service as well as expanded programs of instruction in colleges, theological schools and seminaries.

The approach to society at large should be made by establishing dynamic and cooperative associations with every segment of the community: business, labor, education, government, the professions, and voluntary citizen groups. The effort here should be to insure that all necessary facilities and services are available to help individuals to adjust to the new circumstances in which they find themselves with the approach of old age. In addition, religious congregations should work for legislation and industrial practices which contribute to the orderly transition from active employment to retirement and a useful old age. Churches and synagogues, having expressed their concern for counseling and psychotherapeutic services for the aged, should work likewise for such services where needed.

CONCLUSION

Religion, in its teaching, ritual and organization, is uniquely equipped to guide and aid men in making the closing years of life a time of deepening fulfillment. To this end, it must remind itself and the entire community that the goal is not to keep the aging busy but to help them find in every moment an opportunity for greatness. At the same time, it must always insist that "the test of a people is how it behaves toward the old," remembering with gratitude the contributions that have been made as well as the problems inherited.

Religion can assist the aging in finding within themselves and in the fellowship of faith the resources to meet those problems and fears which seem inevitably to accompany one's latter years. In illness, trouble, and infirmity as well as in hours of joy and exultation, the community of faith offers strength, comfort and benediction in many forms. Religion binds a man to creation and the Creator, and enables him to face the future with hope. This group summons, then, the great religious bodies of the nation, their congregations, seminaries, organizations, and related agencies, and all Americans who share their concern for the aged, to join in expanded efforts toward seeing that each of our senior citizens receives the benefits, spiritual and material, he richly deserves.

NOTE: Quotations in the body of this statement are taken from a paper, "The Older Person and the Family in the Perspective of Jewish Tradition," presented by Professor Abraham J. Heschel at the White House Conference on Aging.

SUGGESTIONS FOR FURTHER STUDY

OUR OLD AGE PROBLEM has vast dimensions and the evidence on every hand indicates that, if present trends continue, it will become more acute with time. Research findings concerning the relationship of church experiences to adjustment or well-being in old age have been examined in this book. These studies led to the major conclusion that religious experiences do play an important role in the personal adjustment of older people. For this reason, knowledge about the older person and the church can be expected to become a major area of gerontology, the science of old age.

This volume provides an orientation and framework for further studies in this area which could contribute much to the understanding and alleviation of the problems of old age. To be sure, there is a relative paucity of knowledge upon which to base such research. Pollak's 1948 declaration still has substantial validity. He said that in the field of religion "changes affecting the participation of older people . . . have received so little attention that the fund of relevant knowledge is hardly sufficient to serve as a basis for making specific research proposals. For the time being, therefore, investigatory efforts . . . will have to be largely exploratory."[1] The situation has improved since that time, but not as greatly as most social scientists, churchmen and older people would desire.

On the basis of the work that has been done to date, a series of subjects on which research could be done in the future to clarify the relationship between religion, especially organized religion or the church, and adjustment in old age are suggested in this section. These will serve a double purpose: (1) They indicate some of the limitations of the knowledge summarized in this book, and (2) they are intended to stimulate the building up of knowledge for the mutual benefit of scientists and churchmen, older people and those who will some day be old, and members of the professions as well as laymen.

1. *Comparative study of additional groups of older church members and non-members.* People living in their own homes could be

1. Otto Pollak, *Social Adjustment in Old Age,* Social Science Research Council, Bulletin 59, 1948, p. 153.

analyzed to supplement the detailed findings presented in Chapter 4 about institutionalized groups of older people. People in other parts of our own nation as well as in foreign lands should likewise be studied.

2. *Evaluative studies of various types of church programs.* How do church-related programs designed specifically for older people affect them spiritually, socially and psychologically? Everything the church does has some effect upon its older constituents. What is the impact of the youth programs stressed so keenly by many churches upon their older members? What is contributed to them by worship services, programs of the various organizations, and other activities that are church-related? Out of such studies can flow effective programs of religious education. Longitudinal studies with both control and experimental groups measured "before and after" probably are the ideal method to use for this purpose. These would include analysis of the needs to be served, the objectives of the programs introduced, and the leadership responsible for carrying them out in the particular community and institutional settings.

3. *Differences between church members of varying social classes.* It is common knowledge that there are significant differences between people on the various social and economic levels. It is probable that the position of older church people in the class structure is related to their personal and social adjustment in old age. In fact, it is even possible that the concept of "personal adjustment" is class-oriented and that new measuring concepts and tools will be needed to discover some of the differences of well-being between the members of differing social classes.

4. *The impact of urbanization upon the church and its older members.* Comparisons of older people in rural and urban churches and of rural-to-urban migrants with non-migrants might provide a basis for prediction of what might be the result of the constantly increasing urbanization of our nation. Problems thus indicated could become a focus for corrective action by the churches.

5. *Religious conflict and personal adjustment in old age.* What are the subjective and objective results of the competitive striving of younger and older church members? How do church splits affect the participants when they reach old age, whether soon or long after the divisions? How many older people have been driven away from the church and religion as a result of internal conflict in the church? How many have emerged from them with strengthened faith and improved personal adjustment?

6. *Personal satisfactions provided the older person by religion and the church.* Additional empirical investigations of the role of religion in times of personal crisis could contribute to our understanding both of the role of the church in modern society and of the social-psychological mechanisms of behavior of older people. What changes in the conception of self result from changes in status in the

church in old age? How does religion help alleviate feelings of loneliness, anxieties about death and the loss of a sense of usefulness?
How does it help the older person maintain or regain a feeling of
self-respect, companionship and faith in the future? Probing into
these subjective areas may not be possible except through long and
skillful exploration of individuals selected because they are able to
verbalize their inner feelings more freely than the average older
person.

7. *Self-selection of religious faith and activity.* It is possible that
those who are religious are better adjusted in old age than those who
are not because those who are well-adjusted are more likely to be
religious. In other words, being "well-adjusted" and being "religious"
may be common effects of some other cause, and the two may not be
directly connected in a causal way to each other. If poorly adjusted
persons do become deeply religious, what changes, if any, take place
in their lives? If any well-adjusted individuals could be found who
have given up their religion in old age, the effects of this change
could be studied. The controlled study of the selection of certain
types of religious activities by older people and their rejection by
others would make a significant contribution to our knowledge and
would have both theoretical and practical significance.

8. *The relationship between non-Christian religions and personal
adjustment in old age.* Most of the findings reported in this book
relate to various types of the Christian religion in our own culture.
Judaism in its various forms, Buddhism, Hinduism, and other religions could be analyzed both from the philosophical-theoretical
viewpoint and from the standpoint of the practical hypotheses that
would emerge from theological analyses. Such studies could be made
in varying types of social settings in which these are found, as, of
course, is also the case with Christianity.

9. *Religion and personal adjustment in the various stages of the
cycle of adjustment.* As an individual passes through the stages in
the cycle of adjustment, it is possible that religion has different
meaning and significance at the various social and psychological
phases.[2] The assumed contributions of religion to personal adjustment may operate with either accelerating or decelerating speed as
time elapses after the initial or the most outstanding experiences of
the individual with religion. The dynamics of the life-long process
need to be analyzed by longitudinal studies.

10. *The role of adaptability in old age.* Adaptability may be
the key to the observed relationships between religion and personal
adjustment in old age. The adaptable person may be the one who
remains happy while the unadaptable one becomes maladjusted with

2. Cf. Ernest W. Burgess, "The Growing Problem of Aging," in Clark
Tibbitts, Editor, *Living Through the Older Years,* University of Michigan
Press, 1949, pp. 17-18.

the loss of occupational, social and economic status that so generally characterizes getting old in our society. If religion increases the adaptability of the older person, it may be responsible for the better adjustment of religious people.

11. *The pervasiveness of religion in old age.* To what extent does religion touch every area of life — economic, marital, occupational, political, social, etc. — and what is its influence? Are some areas more significantly related to the adjustment of the individual than others? How can the most good be done for older people with the least effort?

12. *The "faith of our fathers" and personal adjustment in old age.* Is the best personal adjustment in old people today found among those who conform to the types of religious faith and practice that were taught them in their childhood and youth? If so, what does this mean for a generation reared in a different religious atmosphere?

13. *Leadership in the church and satisfactions in later maturity.* Sociometric analysis could be used to single out the true leaders in the church, regardless of whether or not they are office-holders. The effects of loss of office could be analyzed for both the true leaders and those who were merely office-holders on a comparative basis. The process of losing office in the later years of life and its effects upon personal adjustment at various stages in the process is also worthy of study.

14. *Comparison of church participation and other social participation.* It is possible that the relationships observed between church participation and good personal adjustment in old age are a result of the social participation and would accrue to the individuals involved in any other type of organizational affiliation and activity. Do lodges, clubs and other voluntary organizations perform the same functions for older people as the church? What implications follow from findings either in support of or contrary to this hypothesis? Are they the same for the married as for widowed, divorced, separated and single persons?

15. *The status of older people in the church.* There is some evidence that older people in the church generally are in a position of subjection and subordination. Yet it is possible that they are often "the power behind the throne" even when they do not hold positions of leadership in old age. If so, they may have much more influence in our religious institutions than is generally conceded. The extent to which this is true and the reasons why it is or is not so would be worth investigation both for its own sake and for its implications for gerontological research in other institutions and segments of our society. The place of older people in phases of church activity other than leadership is also a worthy subject of study.

16. *The church and the needs of old people.* Much evidence is given in this book of the work the church can do for older people.

As the needs of the aged become increasingly clear, it may be discovered that some needs which the church is not now meeting can best be satisfied by it and that some services it is now providing could be offered much more effectively, economically and efficiently by other institutions.

17. *Religious conversions of older people.* Under what circumstances do religious conversions of the aged take place? It is possible that when they occur, they are largely an outgrowth of the frustrations and problems of old age. Knowledge of their frequency, compared to conversions at other ages with populations held constant, would help to confirm or to break down many stereotyped ideas of church workers. Evangelists and the clergy would profit from knowing which types of evangelistic outreach and appeal are most effective among older people.

18. *Fluctuations in the personal adjustment of older people.* The reliability of the Burgess-Cavan-Havighurst Attitudes Inventory (referred to in Chapters 3 and 4) as an instrument to measure personal adjustment in old age has been fairly well established. Yet it is possible that the personal adjustment of an individual as measured by it and similar instruments may vary somewhat with such factors as the weather. When it is cloudy and dreary, many elderly folks long for the sun. In certain kinds of weather, arthritic pains are more severe. Similarly, after a discouraging experience in the church, the individual may be despondent. How stable are the feelings of well-being of older people in relation to environmental influences and religious experiences?

19. *Religious beliefs of older people.* In Chapter 3 some evidence is presented that the religious beliefs of the aged as a whole tend to deviate somewhat from those of younger people. Detailed historical, sociological, and psychological analyses of the scope of these differences, and especially of the reasons for them, could help answer the question of whether these observed differences are primarily an outgrowth of the aging process or a result of divergent experiences and varying exposure to religion in childhood, youth and adulthood.

20. *International comparisons.* Are the findings of the relationships between religion and adjustment in old age reported in this book limited to our own culture? Different findings may emerge from studies in nations dominated by a state church or in those with some one dominant religious organization. Research on this subject could be related to other, more extensive studies of the advantages and disadvantages of free-church and established-church societies.

CONCLUSION

The discriminating reader will undoubtedly observe that many of these suggestions for further research and study overlap. Any comprehensive, large-scale project of research on the church and the older person would have to consider many, if not all, of these, and they would of necessity have to be interdisciplinary in scope.   Smaller studies could be made, of course, on any suggested topic.

These suggestions are not an encyclopedic or exhaustive presentation of all projects that are possible.   Rather, they are intended to be suggestive and stimulating to those who are interested in this field of knowledge as scientists, "social engineers," or church workers concerned either with theoretical problems or programs of action.

INDEX

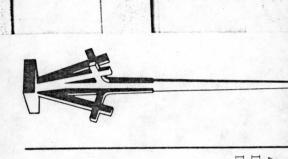

David A. Wright
Director of Library Se

ADDITIONAL ENTRIES